Jack the Ripper

www.pocketessentials.com

Other books in this series by Mark Whitehead:

Slasher Movies
Roger Corman
Animation

Jack the Ripper

MIRIAM RIVETT & MARK WHITEHEAD

POCKET ESSENTIALS

This edition published in 2006 by Pocket Essentials
P.O.Box 394, Harpenden, Herts, AL5 1XJ
www.pocketessentials.com

A CIP catalogue record for this book is available from the British
Library.

ISBN 10: 1 904048 69 2
ISBN 13: 978 1 904048 69 5

2 4 6 8 10 9 7 5 3 1

Typeset by Avocet Typeset, Chilton, Aylesbury, Bucks
Printed and bound in Spain

For Ian and Joel, who put up with endless
Ripper discussions,
and for Meryl, who knew it all already.

Acknowledgements

Our thanks to Paul, Ion and David, for patience, encouragement and books (you all know which). We would also like to extend our thanks to Philip Sugden, Paul Begg, Martin Fido, Keith Skinner, Stewart P Evans, Donald Rumbelow and Ross Strachan, whose research and diligence aided our own work invaluably.

Contents

CONTENTS

Introduction
The Trouble with Jack

'I was killing when killing wasn't cool'

Al Columbia

'In this business no one knows anything'

William Goldman

You might not have heard of Amelia Dyer. In the late 1880s this ex-Salvation Army 'soldier' fostered orphaned infants. While she collected their boarding fees, she swiftly disposed of her charges by strangling and dumping them in the Thames. She was known as 'The Reading Baby Farmer'.

Nor may you have heard of Herman Webster Mudgett (aka HH Holmes). Mudgett ran a hotel in Chicago which benefited in more ways than one from the 1893 World's Fair. A gothic eyesore, the place was a massive killing jar, full of secret entrances, trapdoors and hidden rooms. By the time the police twigged, Holmes had fled. Estimates of the dead found range from twenty-seven to over two hundred.

Or Rhynwick Williams. In 1790, he was arrested and tried as the 'London Monster'. With over fifty victims to his name, the Monster had been the terror of London women from 1788. He approached them with lascivious talk then slashed their buttocks with a knife.

Other names do stick in the mind. Brady and Hindley,

Peter Sutcliffe, Fred and Rose West. They remain in our collective consciousness, their memory sustained by tabloid hysteria and broadsheet pontificating. Their victims' lives have been chronicled exhaustively through oral tradition, the media and by noted authors. The murderers' lives continue to be scrutinised, each new event a source of outrage and discussion. All of it feeds our curiosity about Those Who Did What We Would Never Do. When Fred West committed suicide, it was a cause for populist, pun-filled celebration ('Happy Noose Year!' – *The Sun*, the day after West hanged himself in jail).

And that's the real reason that they remain ever present. It's not outrage or grieving over the victims that really shift units or fill column inches. No matter how liberal we try to be, one word remains (and it's not 'monster'). The word is: Why?

There is a desire to understand what motivates such crimes. There has to be a reason, there just has to be. The detective approaches the subject by deductive reasoning, by using the grey cells – whodunnits tell us this is so. They must know the motive to know the killer. The killer gets an opportunity to tie up any loose ends before they are led away. The motives are always there in a nebulous form: power, sex, boredom, money. These are universal things that tie us to Them. But it's never the Reason. That's personal, the collision of countless moments in time, emotions, desires, beliefs and the indefinable. Something We could never understand.

And still we search.

There's another name that might just ring a bell. He remains in our collective consciousness, subject to occasional tabloid outbursts. His victims' lives have been chronicled exhaustively over the past hundred-odd years. The murderer's many, many possible lives continue to be scrutinised. Each new discovery about him is greeted with heated discussion. All of it feeds our curiosity about The One That Never Got Caught. Jack the Ripper. It is the perfect name for a villain. It is probably too perfect. The letters that gave him his name are most likely hoaxes perpetrated by a journalist wanting to boost sales, but the name remains. We know the name before we ever know anything about the case. It's as if we've been born with that name in our heads, part of our common mythology. It's all part of the trouble with Jack.

Jack, familiar name for John, a name of fairy tales and legends – Jack the Giant Killer, Jack and Jill, Jack-Be-Nimble… Jolly Jack Tar (well, the Ripper was often described as wearing a sailor's hat). London, no stranger to crimes or legends, had already been visited by one malevolent Jack in the 1800s. Spring-Heeled Jack, a fire-breathing, metal-taloned monster capable of prodigious leaps, who attacked bewildered London suburb dwellers. His reign of terror from 1838 to around 1904 saw him enshrined in nursery folklore as a bogeyman and as a popular figure for the penny dreadfuls. Curiously, just as the new Jack moved into London, the old one was spotted in Liverpool.

The Ripper? Well, he certainly ripped up his victims, and several suspects were claimed to have threatened to rip up people. Late 19th-century slang already used the word to mean both 'a first-rate man' and 'a person who behaves badly.' So was the name meant as a clue? Or was it used because it sounded cool or frightening? That's the trouble with Jack. Everything has been analysed to the nth degree, everyone knows too much and yet no one knows anything.

Each new theory pores over the same details, the same cold entrails, searching for meaning, for an identity to leap out. Princes are named, doctors, writers, sailors. A game of cherry stones would be an equally useful divining tool. The trouble with Jack is that we can only build up his appearance through other people's perceptions and experiences. What he did to his victims and the mixed descriptions of the sightings of men with the victims are continually cited. Everything is coloured by press reports, the public's reactions, the police's inability to find so much as a trace of him and the memoirs and theories that paint many different pictures. Even by Hollywood. A man of medium build with a curled-up moustache and a sailor's hat. A top-hatted, caped toff with a little black bag sweeping through a pea-souper. The devil himself. Jack shifts and morphs in our imagination the more that we read. And that's without his supposed diary.

The lies that surround him are enough to send anyone mad: He removed Kelly's foetus (she wasn't pregnant), he fed his victims poisoned grapes (greengrocer Matthew Packer, the only witness to this fact, changed his story every day), he left ritualistic patterns of the victims' belongings near the corpses (nope), and so on and on. Stephen Knight quotes *The Protocols of the Elders of Zion* (an early 20th-century anti-Semitic hoax) as being Masonic oaths. Donald McCormick dramatises scenes, complete with Cockney sing-songs, but insists that the dialogue is authentic. Jonathan Goodman named 'Peter J Harpick' as a suspect, complete with background and history in his book *Who He?*

(1984). Although this was clearly an anagram, requests for further information about 'Harpick' over the years left Goodman with a low opinion of Ripper enthusiasts. AP Wolf starts by claiming Ripperologists' infighting has obscured all truth behind the Ripper case and then savages Colin Wilson. Paul Feldman as good as invites anyone who doubts the veracity of Maybrick's diary outside for a fight. The myth sucks you in. Each step you take pulls you harder, deeper. You fight your corner by whatever means necessary, because you, and you alone, have The Truth.

The truth? The incredible police investigation into the crimes derived not from sympathy for the victims but from politics. In 1876, corruption on a massive scale had been uncovered in the higher echelons of the CID. The Metropolitan Police, under Sir Charles Warren, were regarded as an increasingly militaristic force. The press, previously in favour of the forces of law and order cracking down on the unruly poor, suddenly began to support those they had vilified. The police in all areas had to be seen to prove themselves.

Jack was born just as the popular press was finding its feet and they helped each other immeasurably. He gave them murders to boost their circulation and they, in turn, made him into a legend. No detail was too titillating or unpleasant to be left unreported or undistorted. Researchers hoping to provide a correct history of the murders are left with the daunting task of sorting the lies from the truth through acres of print, reports, statements... The coroner, Wynne Baxter, held lengthy inquests into many of the victims. These supplied the press with every possible detail of the victims' backgrounds, their murders, their mutilations. Gaudy posters advertising the latest reports from the press were pasted up around Whitechapel, saturating the people of the area in the deeds of the monster. Peter Turnbull in *The Killer Who Never Was* (1996) suggests that the Ripper was a product of such heightened awareness. The hysteria that greeted each crime, fuelled by so much information, created copycat killers, each of whom murdered another prostitute and further fanned the flames. One theory amongst hundreds. But it happens. The 'Halifax Slasher' of 1938 was the product of such increasing hysteria. Women were found to have slashed themselves and blamed a mystery assailant. It is entirely likely that the reign of The London Monster contains similar elements. But these were phantom crimes. The trouble with Jack is that there really were murders. Someone did it. Whether a legion of copycats or a single-minded individual, someone did it. We have the bodies, and the same constantly reproduced photographs to prove it. Tabram, Nichols, Chapman and Stride, just sleeping. Eddowes naked, bloody, propped up and sewn up, empty. Kelly at rest, Manet's *Olympia* adapted by the Chapman Brothers.

So who was Jack? We have no more idea than you do. Pick a suspect. MJ Trow showed how easy it is to make anyone fit the Ripper's clothes in his essay *The Way to Hell* (1999). Pick a name and then find the isolated incidents in his (or even her) life that you can bend to your theory. We have no new theories to propose and no new names to put forward. What you find here are the speculations of other, more qualified people, members of that driven breed, the Ripper researchers. We tip our hats to them. The facts contained in this book are, hopefully, the essentials – compared and distilled from their work to bring you an overview of the

Ripper's reign of terror and of the women that he murdered.

They did not die in vain. Jack is accredited with instigating social reform where others had failed. The highest in the land were regularly informed of the state of the poor. Even Queen Victoria sent letters to the police, offering suggestions as to how the killer might be traced. Whitechapel, the labyrinthine immigrant quarter so close to the City, home to 80,000 forgotten people, became front-page news. The reports drew attention to the neglected, the poor and, at the bottom of the social ladder, the extreme poor, forced to sleep in doorways, to beg or sell themselves for fourpence for their doss in one of the 233 overcrowded common lodging houses. Between them these houses accommodated around 8,500 people. Despite the frequent cries of 'Murder!' which most witnesses remarked on and ignored, and despite the brutality and violence which thrived in the area, not one of the 80 murders committed in London the previous year had occurred in Whitechapel. Jack's victims, drawn from 'the unfortunates' (the polite euphemism for prostitutes), raised the profile of the area as no reformer had done before. George Bernard Shaw went so far as to acknowledge the Ripper as achieving what he and fellow socialists had failed to do. This said, Jack London's *The People of the Abyss* (1902), relating his time spent living amongst the extreme poor of the East End, revealed that little had been done to alleviate the suffering in the area fifteen years after the Whitechapel Murders.

Sexual maniac, proto-serial killer, social reformer, black humorist, man of a thousand faces... The trouble with Jack, ultimately, is that the more you read about him, the more his stature as a legendary figure grows. At some point the masks have to be removed. Not to reveal his identity. That bearpit remains. Stripped of his iconic veneer, Jack is just a murderer. Someone who found women who had no other option but to sell their bodies then strangled and mutilated them. Not a devil. Not a ghost. Not a black magician endowed with supernatural powers. An ordinary person, one of the crowd, like you or I. Someone who could pass without let or hindrance through the East End streets with no one noticing his presence as being out of the ordinary.

The trouble with Jack is getting people to realise that.

In Hindsight

> 'Vice can afford to pay more than honesty, but its prof-
> its at last go to landlords.'
>
> Reverend Samuel Barnett, letter to The Times,
19 September 1888.

Emma Smith

Sometime between 4 and 5am on 3 April 1888, Emma
Smith returned to lodgings at 18, George Street,
Spitalfields. She told the house's deputy keeper, Mary
Russell, that she had been assaulted and robbed in Osborn
Street (about 300 yards away). Smith, a 45-year-old prostitute, had lived at George Street for 18 months and was
known for returning at all hours, usually drunk. That night,
she had been returning from a night's soliciting at 1.30am
when three men had attacked her outside Taylor Bros Cocoa
factory near Brick Lane.

Russell and Annie Lee, a lodger, escorted her to London
Hospital where she was attended by house surgeon Dr
George Haslip. As well as bruising to her face and a torn
right ear, Smith's vagina had been penetrated by a blunt
object so forcefully that it had ruptured her peritoneum.
Peritonitis resulted. After slipping into a coma, she died at
9am on 4 April.

Despite probably passing several policemen during her

journeys to and from George Street, Smith had not reported the incident, or asked for assistance. Officers on patrol that evening said that they hadn't seen or heard anything unusual. The police were not alerted to the attack on Smith until they were informed that a coroner's inquest was to be held on 7 April.

Wynne Baxter presided over the inquest at the London Hospital. Baxter would conduct inquests into six other Whitechapel murders associated with the Ripper. Known for his flashy dress and, later, his friction with the Metropolitan Police, Baxter had become coroner for East London and Tower of London in 1887 after a bitter election contest. At the inquest an anonymous witness testified to having seen Smith at around a quarter past midnight near Burdett Road (about two miles from where she was attacked), talking to 'a man dressed in dark clothes with a white neckerchief'. The witness had been hurrying away from the area since she had been assaulted by two men a few minutes before she saw Smith. One man had asked her the time and the other had struck her in the mouth before both ran away. The witness didn't think that the man talking to Smith had been one of these.

Also present at the inquest was Chief Inspector John West of H Division. West would become acting Superintendent during the murder investigations of Mary Ann Nichols and Annie Chapman, and be responsible for combining the enquiries into the Whitechapel murders under Inspector Abberline. At this point, West had no official information on the assault.

The jury's verdict was 'Wilful murder by some person or persons unknown'. Unofficially, it was believed that Smith had been killed by members of a band of street thugs from

The Nichol, a slum area near Old Nichol Street at the top of Brick Lane. The gang's preferred livelihood consisted of extracting protection money from East End prostitutes and it was possible that they'd brutalised Smith as a warning to other women to pay up or suffer similar treatment.

Martha Tabram

Martha Tabram (aka Martha Turner, Emma Turner) was the ex-wife of Henry Samuel Tabram, foreman packer at a furniture warehouse. They'd had two sons but separated in 1875 because of Martha's excessive drinking. By 1879 she was living with Henry Turner, a street hawker. He too found Martha's drinking difficult to cope with. As a result they often spent periods apart and finally separated in July 1888. Martha supported herself through prostitution and selling trinkets on the streets. During this time, she took lodgings at 19, George Street, Spitalfields, living there under the name Emma Turner. On Saturday 4 August 1888, Martha met Turner in Leadenhall Street where he gave her money to buy some more trinkets to sell. It was the last time that he saw her.

The following Monday, Martha went out for the evening with Mary Ann Connolly (also known as 'Pearly Poll'). According to Connolly they met two guardsmen, a corporal and a private, in The Two Brewers pub, most likely situated in Brick Lane. They drank with their new-found acquaintances in various other pubs, including the White Swan in Whitechapel High Street until about 11.45pm when they paired off to have sex. Connolly and the corporal went to Angel Alley (situated next to Osborn Street), while Martha and the private went into George Yard (now Gunthorpe

Street). The buildings there were relatively new (constructed in 1875) but cheap, single-room dwellings, occupied by the poorest in the area.

At around 2.00am, PC Thomas Barrett was patrolling the area. He encountered a soldier he later described as being a Grenadier Guardsman. The soldier was in his early-to-late twenties, 5 feet 9 inches tall, with a fair complexion, dark hair and a small brown moustache turned up at the ends. The man was loitering in Wentworth Street. He claimed he was 'waiting for a chum who had gone with a girl'. Barrett later stated he would recognise the soldier, a private, if he saw him again. This he was later asked to do.

Arriving home at 3.30am, a cab driver, Albert Crow, came across a body on the first-floor landing of George Yard buildings. He thought it was a tramp sleeping rough, a regular occurrence in the area. At 4.45am in the same block, John Reeves, a waterside labourer, left his home to seek work. He also saw the body on the landing but was more observant than Crow. He saw that it was a woman lying on her back in a pool of blood. He immediately sought a police officer and found PC Barrett, who sent for a doctor. Barrett noted that the woman's clothes were 'turned up as far as the centre of the body' leaving the lower half exposed as if 'recent intimacy had taken place'. At the coroner's inquest, Reeves testified that he hadn't seen any footprints or blood leading to the body, or any sign of a weapon.

The doctor called to the scene, Dr Timothy Killeen, arrived around 5.30am, and estimated that the woman had been dead for three hours. She had been stabbed 39 times. As there was no public mortuary in Whitechapel the police took the body to the workhouse infirmary in Old Montague

Street. Killeen conducted the post-mortem, finding wounds to both lungs, the heart, liver, spleen and stomach as well as the breasts and genital area. He concluded that most of the wounds had been inflicted by a right-handed assailant and that all the wounds bar one could have been inflicted by an ordinary penknife. However, one wound penetrated the sternum, and Killeen thought that this must have been inflicted by a dagger or possibly a bayonet. Whether this wound had been caused by another assailant, Killeen did not speculate, but he contended that it was possibly made by a left-handed person unlike the others. It has been pointed out that he may have been unaware that the standard-issue triangular bayonet had been withdrawn from issue the previous year and that the blade replacing it could well have made all of the wounds.

At the coroner's inquest on 9 August, the deputy coroner for south-east Middlesex, George Collier (Wynne Baxter was on holiday) remained hopeful that the body would be identified. Three women had come forward but identified the dead woman under three different names. The inquest was adjourned for a fortnight. On 14 August, Henry Tabram, Martha's ex-husband, positively identified her. He'd only learned of her death when he noticed the name Tabram mentioned in one of the newspaper reports of the murder.

Meanwhile, Mary Ann Connolly had come forward to give details of Martha's last night. On 9 August, she told the police at Commercial Street station that she could identify both soldiers if she saw them again. An identity parade of corporals and privates in the Grenadier Guards who had been on leave that evening was assembled at the Tower of London the following day. Connolly failed to show. Later traced by the police to her cousin's house in Drury Lane,

Connolly was taken to a second identity parade at the Tower on 13 August, but failed to identify the men. She now said that they'd had white bands around their caps, which suggested they were Coldstream Guards. A similar parade was assembled at Wellington Barracks, Birdcage Walk on 15 August. Here Connolly picked out Guardsmen George and Skipper, both of whom had strong alibis. Let down once more by 'Pearly Poll,' the police did not seek her questionable assistance any further.

PC Barrett also attended identity parades at the Tower. On 8 August he picked out two men. Later, Barrett admitted his first choice was wrong (this private wore medals whereas the man Barrett encountered on the 7th wore none). The second, Private John Leary, had been drinking with Private Law in Brixton until closing time. Losing Law, Leary had returned via Battersea and Chelsea, meeting up with Law once more in the Strand at about 4.30am. They had reached barracks around 6.00am. Law corroborated Leary's statement.

Inspector Edmund Reid of H Division CID organised the identity parades and questioned those guards picked out by Connolly and Barrett. In his report dated 24 September 1888 he concludes: 'Having both picked out the wrong men they could not be trusted again as their evidence would be worthless.'

The time lapse between Tabram's disappearance with the guardsman (11.45pm) and her estimated time of death (2.30am) seems curious. It is certainly possible that she found another client after the private. It may also be possible that the soldier PC Barrett saw at 2.00am was not the same one that Connolly had been with earlier. Further to this, Private Law could only corroborate that part of Private

Leary's story for which he was present. However, Barrett's confusion over identification obviously made Inspector Reid doubtful of his powers of recollection. The inquest reconvened on 23 August. The verdict returned was one of 'Wilful murder by some person or persons unknown'. It was a verdict that would recur over the coming months.

Tabram's ferocious murder had incited public reaction and led to the establishment of the first of several vigilance committees. St Jude's Vigilance Committee comprised seventy local men and students from Toynbee Hall. Twelve of their group were selected to patrol in the area between 11pm and 1am. In addition, on 18 August, the East London Advertiser reported that the Whitechapel Board of Works had approved 'lamps with double the illuminating power be fixed at the corner of the following streets, viz. – Wentworth Street west corner, Thrawl Street, Flower and Dean Street, Vine Court, Quaker Street, Worship Square'. Attempts to make the area safer were beginning but no one could know how much more unsafe the East End was about to become. The murders were treated as isolated incidents and prostitutes continued to ply their trade on the Whitechapel streets.

As with all the 'canonical' Ripper murders no one was ever apprehended for the killing of Emma Smith or Martha Tabram. Several theorists suggest that Martha Tabram's murder marked the start of Jack the Ripper's career. Both attacks were later linked to the Ripper's crimes by the press but, at the time, horrendous though the crimes were, neither was seen as being part of a pattern. Violence was commonplace in the East End but even so these murders were out of the ordinary.

'Watchman, Old Man, I Believe Somebody Is Murdered Down the Street'

'They were locked together like a famous football team: they were inseparable. Part of the doctrine'
Iain Sinclair, *White Chappell, Scarlet Tracings*

Mary Ann Nichols

For most of its length, Buck's Row (now Durward Street) was a narrow and poorly-lit street. It ran between Brady Street to the east and Baker's Row (now Vallance Street) to the west, both of which joined with Whitechapel Road to the south. From the Brady Street entrance its left-hand side was flanked by a row of run-down two-storey houses mainly occupied by working-class tenants. Next to these there was a stable yard and a board school. After these, Buck's Row widened considerably, meeting with Winthrop Street.

At about 3.40am on the morning of 31 August, carman (cart driver) Charles Cross was walking to work at Pickford's in Broad Street from his home in Bethnal Green. Entering Buck's Row from the east, he was on the right-hand side of the street when he noticed something lying out-side the gate to the stable yard. At first he thought someone had abandoned a tarpaulin but then he realised that he was mistaken. It was the body of a woman.

Uncertain what to do, Cross was shortly joined by

another carman, Robert Paul, on his way to work in Spitalfields. Together they went to examine the body. She was lying on her back, her skirts raised almost to her stomach. Cross felt her hands and told Paul: 'I think she is dead.' Putting his hand on her heart, Paul was not so certain. 'I think she is breathing,' he replied, 'but very little if she is.' He asked Cross to help him prop her up, but Cross refused. In the darkness they could see little of what might have caused the woman's condition and, after an attempt to pull her skirts down, they headed off towards Baker's Row in search of a policeman. At the corner of Baker's Row and Hanbury Street they met PC Jonas Mizen and told him of their discovery. 'I think she is dead or drunk,' Cross told him. Mizen went to investigate and the two men, unwilling to lose more time, went their separate ways.

Meanwhile, the body had been discovered by another policeman. At 3.45am, PC John Neil's patrol took him east into Buck's Row. With his lantern he was able to examine the woman more closely than it had been possible for the two carmen to do. Her hands were open at her sides, the left touching the stable yard gate, her eyes were open, as was her throat from which blood was oozing. Neil felt her right arm and found it was still warm above the elbow. With his lantern, he signalled PC John Thain from Brady Street. Thain was dispatched to fetch Dr Rees Llewellyn from 152, Whitechapel Road. Neil was joined shortly by PC Mizen, who went to fetch an ambulance (basically a wheeled stretcher) and assistance from Bethnal Green police station.

Neil rang the bell at Essex Wharf (across the road from the stable yard) and asked if anyone had heard a disturbance.

Neither the manager, Walter Purkiss, nor his wife had heard anything, despite having had a restless night's sleep. Further enquiries were made by Sergeant Kerby, who had arrived at the same time as Dr Llewellyn. Kerby enquired at the house of Mrs Emma Green, who lived with her daughter and two sons at the first of the houses on Buck's Row. None of them had noticed anything unusual during the night.

Dr Llewellyn's on-site examination confirmed that the woman was dead and had been, he estimated, for about half an hour. Although there was very little blood around her, or in the gutter nearby, there were no bloodstains to suggest that the body had been dragged there. Neither was there any evidence of a struggle. Llewellyn ordered the woman to be removed to Old Montague Street Workhouse infirmary mortuary, where he would make a further examination.

At the inquest Thain, Mizen and Neil would tell how, once the body had been moved, a patch of congealed blood was revealed, about six inches in diameter. More, however, had been absorbed by the woman's clothes. PC Thain found, when lifting her onto the stretcher, that her back was covered with blood which smeared his hands.

Mizen, Neil and Kerby escorted the body to the mortuary. After visiting the crime scene, Inspector Spratling, divisional inspector of J Division, arrived at the mortuary to find it locked up and the body on the stretcher in the yard. While he waited for Robert Mann, the keeper of the mortuary, to arrive, he took a description of the woman. Mann arrived between 5.00 and 5.20am whereupon the body was taken inside. It was there that Spratling summoned Dr Llewellyn once more for, lifting the woman's clothes, he found that the wound to her throat was the least of their concerns. Her abdomen had been viciously ripped open up to the sternum and her intestines exposed.

Dr Llewellyn's post-mortem noted the following: There were lacerations to the tongue. Bruises to both sides of the jaw were probably caused by pressure from a thumb and fingers. There were two deep incisions in the neck, the second and longest of which cut right down to the vertebrae. There were no wounds to the body above the deep, jagged wound to the abdomen on the left and several similar cuts to the abdomen on the right. All of these were inflicted violently downwards and from left to right, 'as might have been done by a left-handed person'. He concluded: 'All the injuries had been caused by the same instrument.' No part of the viscera was missing. Later, he would express doubts about his original supposition that the murderer was left-handed.

Identifying the victim seemed difficult, but within a day her name was revealed and her life began to take shape for the investigators. As news of the latest murder spread through the East End, it transpired that a woman fitting the deceased's description had lodged at 18, Thrawl Street. One occupant, Ellen Holland, identified the body as 'Polly'. A more solid identification resulted from the laundry mark of Lambeth Workhouse in the victim's petticoats. Mary Ann Monk, an inmate of the workhouse, identified the woman as Mary Ann Nichols, 43, who had been at the workhouse as recently as May that year. The police then traced the deceased's father, Edward Walker, and her estranged husband, William Nichols, both of whom identified the body the next day.

Mary Ann Nichols' story, like the inquests' verdicts, was one that would become familiar during the Whitechapel murders. Born in 1845, she had married William in 1864. During their marriage they had five children, three sons and two daughters, between 1866 and 1879. Domestic problems seem to have begun at least as early as 1877 when William briefly eloped with the midwife of their second daughter. Mary Ann began drinking heavily from this time and left home five or six times.

In 1880, the couple separated, with William retaining custody of the children. He paid Mary Ann five shillings in weekly allowance until 1882, when he learned that she was living by prostitution. From September 1880, she spent much time in workhouses, predominantly Lambeth. For two months in 1883, she moved back in with her father, leaving after a quarrel over her drinking. Between June 1883 and October 1887 she lived with Thomas Stuart Drew, a blacksmith, at 15, York Street, Walworth. Little is known about their relationship or why they parted. Her father last saw her in June 1886, when she attended the funeral of her brother, but they did not speak. Between April and June 1888, she was employed by Mr and Mrs Cowdrey in Wandsworth. During this time she wrote to her father attempting to bridge the gap between them. Her father's sympathetic letter in reply brought no response, so he was unaware that she had absconded from her employers on 12 July, stealing clothing worth £3 10 shillings. She began lodging at 18, Thrawl Street on 2 August 1888 where she shared a room with three other women. From 24 August, she stayed at 'The White House' 56, Flower and Dean Street, a doss house which allowed men and women to sleep together.

At 12.30am, on 30 August, she was spotted leaving The Frying Pan public house in Brick Lane. At 1.20am, she attempted to return to 18, Thrawl Street. The deputy keeper described her as 'slightly tipsy' and turned her away because she did not have her 'doss'. Nichols laughed as she left, telling him: 'I'll soon get my doss money; see what a jolly bonnet I've got now.' He did not recall seeing it before. Ellen Holland met her at 2.30am at the corner of Osborn Street and Whitechapel High Street. By this time she was drunk and staggering. She told Ellen that she had earned her doss money three times that day and spent it. Ellen asked her to come back to Thrawl Street with her, but she refused. The next person to see her was her killer.

With Nichols' murder following so closely after Martha Tabram's, the press were quick to link both crimes to the same person and also threw in Emma Smith's death for good measure. The murders of three women in such a small area of the East End did little to dispel this idea and public concern grew. A clothing manufacturer based in Spitalfields sent a newspaper cutting about Nichols' murder to the Home Secretary, Henry Matthews, requesting that a reward be offered for the murderer's capture. The Home Office responded, but only to point out that offering rewards for the capture of criminals 'has for some time been discontinued' and that they saw no reason to review this situation.

At this point Scotland Yard became involved, with the arrival of the man whose name became synonymous with the Ripper case: Inspector Frederick George Abberline. Aged 45, his modest and soft-spoken demeanour belied his years of experience. No photograph of him seems to have survived, but contemporaneous newspaper sketches portray him as a portly figure, balding but with a bushy moustache and sideburns. By the time of the murders he had worked for twenty-five years in the Metropolitan Police, nine of those (between 1878 and 1887) at H Division. His knowledge of Whitechapel, its inhabitants and its criminals made him the ideal candidate to coordinate the investigations between the divisions involved in the cases. He was so well thought of in the area that when he had transferred to Scotland Yard the previous year he had been honoured by Whitechapel citizens and ex-colleagues at a presentation dinner.

However, despite Abberline and H Division's best efforts, no clue as to Mary Ann Nichols' killer was uncovered. Several police officers searched the area, including nearby railway tracks and buildings, but no weapon or clue were found. One possible clue was the sighting of a man who, according to Abberline, 'passed down Buck's Row while the doctor was examining the body'. It is not stated in which direction he was heading. Patrick Mulshaw, a nightwatchman at a sewage works supposedly in Winthrop Street, claimed that a man passed by him sometime after 4.00am. Mulshaw gave no description of the man, other than he had spoken, saying: 'Watchman, old man, I believe somebody is murdered down the street'. As well as being a strikingly odd turn of phrase, it has been noted by researcher John Carey (in *Ripperana* 36) that it also seems strange that the man was heading away from the murder scene, given that general curiosity drew most of those in the area to go and gawp at the body.

Driven to make their own investigations due to police reticence in supplying information, the press sought another man. Local prostitutes had told the police about a man who had, for some time, been demanding money with menaces from them. They called him 'Leather Apron'. Journalists got hold of this information and newspapers, particularly *The Star*, began to carry descriptions of him and his crimes. He was supposedly a Jewish slipper maker with black hair and moustache, aged about 40, wearing a close-fitting cap and, of course, a leather apron. He usually carried a large knife and frequently threatened his victims with the phrase, 'I'll rip you up!' The reports added to this some pure stage villainy: 'His eyes are small and glittering. His lips are usually parted in a grin which is not only not reassuring, but excessively repellent.' At some point the 'monster's' real name became known. He was John Pizer, a Polish Jewish boot finisher. Further gloating press coverage not only helped to convince fearful locals that 'Leather Apron' and the Whitechapel murderer were one and the same, but also stirred up considerable anti-Semitic feeling in the area. Police enquiries concerning his whereabouts uncovered some sightings. Timothy Donovan of Crossingham's Lodging House confirmed that he had seen him there sometime before the murders commenced and had thrown him out for threatening a woman. He was also said to frequent the Princess Alice pub in Commercial Street but now seemed to have vanished. The Police tried to calm the situation, and Inspector Helson's weekly report to Scotland Yard (7 September) said that they were merely trying to find Pizer in order to establish his whereabouts on the night of Nichols' murder for 'at present there is no evidence whatsoever against him'.

The inquest into Nichols' death opened on 1 September. It was held at the Whitechapel Working Lads' Institute and headed by Wynne Baxter. With adjournments it ran over four days (reconvened 3 September, 17 September and 23 September). During his summation, Baxter criticised the police for not noticing the mutilation of the body sooner and complained about the lack of proper mortuary facilities in Whitechapel. Despite the police's best efforts over the previous three weeks, the jury's verdict was 'Wilful murder by some person or persons unknown'. The foreman of the jury commented that if a reward had been offered the killer would probably have been caught. He blamed class bias for, if the victim had been rich, a reward would certainly have been offered.

Nichols was buried on 6 September at the City of London cemetery in Ilford. The mourners included her father, her husband and her eldest son. Police and the undertaker conspired to keep sightseers away so the cortege could leave Whitechapel unhindered.

'Cool Impudence and Reckless Daring'

'Human kind cannot bear very much reality'
T S Eliot, Four Quartets: Burnt Norton

Annie Chapman

One needs look no further than Annie Chapman for a prime example of the misery of those women's lives who crossed Jack the Ripper's path. She was known to many of her acquaintances as 'Dark Annie' – allegedly because of the dark moods that frequently gripped her. Her life certainly gave her good reason. She was born in 1841 to George Smith, a private in the Lifeguards, and Ruth Chapman. Her brother, Fountain Smith, was born in 1861. She supposedly had a sister, of whom little is known, other than Annie mentioning that she lived in Vauxhall. In 1869, Annie married John Chapman, a relative of her mother, at All Saints Church in Knightsbridge. They lived together in west London until 1881 when they moved to Windsor. Chapman is often referred to as a veterinary surgeon (this seems to have come from the inquest testimony of Annie's acquaintance, Amelia Palmer), but he was in fact a domestic head coachman. Reportedly he lost his job due to Annie's dishonesty, but there is no definite evidence of this. They had three children, a son (crippled) and two daughters (one died in 1882 and the other, Anna Georgina, ran away with a travelling circus).

Annie left the family before the daughter's death and returned to London. Here she received an allowance of ten shillings a week from John, but the payment was often sporadic. It ceased altogether with his death in 1886.

The press were quick to blame the marital breakdown on Annie's alcoholism and immorality. However, inquest testimony from acquaintances suggests that she was only occasionally drunk and that she was only an occasional prostitute. More often she survived through hawking her own crochet work, matches and flowers. Also, John Chapman died of dropsy and cirrhosis of the liver, further suggesting that Annie was not entirely to blame.

During 1886, Annie lived at 30, Dorset Street with a sievemaker named, or possibly nicknamed, Jack Sievey. Why they separated is uncertain. From May 1888 Annie lived mainly at Crossingham's Lodging House, 35, Dorset Street where, by all accounts, she got on well with the other lodgers. The only exception was in the last week of August when Annie got into a fight with fellow lodger, Eliza Cooper. Their stories differed wildly, but it was definitely over a man and some money and Annie sustained bruises to her right temple and chest.

About 5 feet tall, stout, with dark wavy brown hair, blue eyes and a thick nose, Annie survived rather than lived. Dr Bagster Phillips who examined her after her death found that she was undernourished and had chronic diseases of the lungs and brain membranes that would soon have killed her if fate hadn't intervened. Amelia Palmer, a friend of Annie's, recalled seeing her on 3 September in Dorset Street where Annie had talked of her ill-health and showed Amelia her bruises. She also discussed the possibility of going hop picking 'if my sister will send me the boots'. The next day, Amelia saw her again, this time near Spitalfields Church. Annie told her that she felt no better and that she might go to the infirmary for a day or two. Amelia asked her if she had had anything to eat. When Annie told her she hadn't even had a cup of tea, Amelia gave her tuppence, telling her not to spend it on rum. The last time she saw Annie was on 7 September. They met in Dorset Street at about 5.00pm. Asking her if she was going to Stratford, Annie told Amelia that she wasn't as she felt 'too ill to do anything'. Coming back that way some ten minutes later, Amelia found Annie still in the same place. 'It's no use giving way,' Annie told her, 'I must pull myself together and get some money or I shall have no lodgings.'

At 7pm Annie was back at Crossingham's where she asked Donovan if she could sit in the kitchen. She told him that she had been in the infirmary although there is no record of her being admitted to either Whitechapel or Spitalfields Workhouse Infirmary. At about 12.12am, she was still in the kitchen, where William Stevens, a fellow lodger, found her 'slightly the worse for drink'. He saw her take a box of pills from her pocket. The box broke and Annie transferred the pills to a piece of torn envelope taken from the floor. At this point, Annie left and probably went for a drink (Frederick Stevens, another lodger, recalled having a pint of beer with her at 12.30am). By 1.35am she had returned to Crossingham's. Donovan claims that he found her drunk and eating a baked potato. A bed was vacant and Donovan asked her for her 'doss'. When told that she didn't have it, Donovan responded that she seemed to find money for drink easily enough. Annie wasn't put out and told him not to let the bed as she would be back for it.

John Evans, the lodging house's nightwatchman, saw her leave. As she left, she said: 'I won't be long, Brummy. See that Tim keeps the bed for me.' He watched her walk into Little Paternoster Row in the direction of Brushfield Street. Evans, too, would state that he thought she was the worse for drink but the likelihood is that he, Stevens and Donovan all took her ill-heath for drunkenness. Her post-mortem would reveal that she hadn't had alcohol for hours. At 5.30am, Elizabeth Darrell (or Durrell) saw a woman whom she identified as Chapman talking with a man outside 29, Hanbury Street. The man had his back to her but she described him as being over forty. Although she did not see his face, Darrell describes him as looking 'like a foreigner', wearing a deerstalker hat, possibly a dark coat and being of 'shabby genteel appearance'. The man asked Chapman, 'Will you?' Chapman replied, 'Yes.'

29, Hanbury Street

29, Hanbury Street was home to seventeen people at the time of Annie Chapman's death. Mrs Amelia Richardson, a widow, was listed as the occupant but she rented out over half of the house and lived in the front room of the first floor with her grandson, Thomas. The cellar and backyard were used for her packing-case manufacturing business in which she was assisted by a man named Francis Tyler and her son, John, who lived in Spitalfields and worked as a porter at the market. The house had a front and back door. Both of these were rarely locked and often left open at night. They were joined by a passageway that ran the length of the house. As a result, people were often found dossing there. Although Mrs Richardson wasn't aware of this, John made it his business to check on the house, usually on days that he was going to market.

On the morning of 8 September, John Richardson checked the house between 4.40 and 4.45am. He went through the passageway and stood on the steps leading into the backyard. Here he paused to cut a piece of leather from his boot that had been chafing his foot. Although he didn't look around thoroughly, he saw nothing in the yard that was out of the ordinary.

At some point between 5.15 and 5.30am (three contemporary sources state three different times) Albert Cadosch (or Cadoche or Cadosh) of 27, Hanbury Street (next door) went into his yard. From behind the fence separating the two houses he heard a conversation between some people in 29's backyard. The only word he caught was a woman saying, 'No'. He did not investigate. Nor was his curiosity piqued when, three minutes later (either 5.18, 5.28 or 5.33) he returned to the yard and heard something fall heavily against the other side of the fence dividing the two properties.

At about 6.00am (on this, most sources seem fairly clear), John Davis, one of 29's many tenants, entered the backyard. It was there that he found the body of Annie Chapman. She was lying on her back, her dress pulled up over her knees and her intestines were placed over her right shoulder. After summoning two men from a nearby packing-case manufacturers, Davis went to fetch the police. Soon the rest of the house was awake, just in time for the police to arrive and secure the building.

At 6.30am, H Division surgeon Dr George Bagster Phillips arrived. According to his on-the-spot examination, Chapman had been dead for two to three hours. Phillips subsequently shortened this period because it was, 'a fairly cool morning and... the body would be more apt to cool rapidly from its having lost a great quantity of blood'. He also noted that the face and tongue were 'very much swollen', suggesting that Chapman had been strangled before being mutilated. Blood smeared on the fence corresponded with where the victim lay, confirming that she had been murdered there.

Phillips' post-mortem notes that Chapman's throat had been severed by a jagged incision. A flap of the stomach wall, the small intestines and attachments had been removed and placed over the right shoulder but remained attached to her body. Two other pieces of stomach wall and sections of her pubic area were placed over the left shoulder. Other parts were missing altogether: a further part of the stomach wall including the navel; the womb; the upper part of the vagina; and most of the bladder. Abrasions on the ring finger suggested that a ring, or rings, had been forcibly removed. Phillips expressed the opinion that, from the removal of viscera, the murderer possessed anatomical knowledge. He believed the knife used was narrow, thin and sharp, with a blade six to eight inches long, 'not an ordinary knife but such as a small amputating knife, or a well-ground slaughterman's knife'. Phillips said he didn't think he could have produced all of Chapman's injuries in under fifteen minutes.

There was friction between Phillips and Wynne Baxter at the inquest. Phillips at first refused to describe the mutilations in great detail because he felt that they would only be 'painful to the feelings of the jury and the public'. On 14 September, Baxter allowed this, but Phillips was recalled five days later when Baxter, after clearing the inquest of all women and boys, insisted that he provided the full details. Phillips did so.

After Chapman's body had been moved, a piece of coarse muslin and a small pocket haircomb case, probably along with two polished farthings were found, seemingly piled up deliberately. A popular con trick was to shine up farthings so that they would pass as shillings in a dim light, but whether Chapman had been going to try this or had had it tried on her remains unknown. Near where her head had been was a portion of an envelope and a piece of paper containing two pills. The back of the envelope bore the Sussex Regiment's seal. On the other side was the letter 'M' in a 'man's' handwriting and the letters 'Sp' (possibly the start of 'Spitalfields'). Postmarked 'London 23 Aug., 1888', some sources quote it as 'London, 28 Aug., 1888'. The envelope came under considerable police scrutiny, and enquiries were made at the Sussex Regiment at Farnborough. However, there was no success in tracing a soldier known to be writing to anyone in Spitalfields. Inspector Chandler would later note, after hearing the statement of William Stevens, that the envelope was most likely the one that Annie Chapman took from the kitchen floor at Crossingham's and therefore not worth pursuing as a possible clue.

Rumours of items deliberately 'arranged' at the other victims' feet have become part of the mythology of Jack the Ripper. But it only happened with Chapman and the items were the contents of her pocket, which had been cut open. The farthings were noted in the newspaper reports of the murder but not mentioned later in the police reports or newspaper reports of the coroner's inquest. Later claims that Chapman's rings were also in the pile are false. In fact, the police spent considerable time checking 'all pawnbrokers, jewellers, dealers' to find the rings that were missing from Chapman's fingers. There were no others found. A search of the backyard revealed some items which were found to belong to Mrs Richardson. More ominously, the police found a sodden leather apron near a tap at the end of the yard. This clue also led nowhere as Mrs Richardson confirmed that it was her son's and had been there since the previous Thursday, when she had washed it.

Like Nichols, Chapman's body was taken to the grimy shed that was Whitechapel Workhouse Infirmary Mortuary for post-mortem. On 9 September, her body was formally identified by both Timothy Donovan and her brother Fountain Smith. On 14 September, she was buried at Manor Park cemetery in a small ceremony attended by family members.

Two days after Chapman's death, the Liberal MP for Whitechapel, Samuel Montagu, personally offered £100 reward for information leading to the murderer's arrest. An advocate of many charities for the poor and particularly immigrant Jews in the East End, he also supported the local Vigilance Committees, forwarding some of their petitions and requests to the Home Office. That same day the Mile End Vigilance Committee was founded by a group of concerned ratepayers. Meeting at The Crown pub in Mile End Road, they elected George Lusk their president, announcing to the press that members would be present in the Crown every morning to hear any information or suggestions that the public had to offer. Lusk later came to fear his new-found publicity.

The inquest into Annie Chapman's death opened on 12 September at the Whitechapel Working Lads' Institute. Presided over by Wynne Baxter, it lasted for five days (reconvened 13, 14, 19 and 26 September), a length which drew criticism. A letter to *The Times* on 19 September, suggested it was time the inquest closed and the usual verdict be given. The amount of information being supplied, the writer remarked, would surely be better used by the police than the press.

When the inquest closed, Baxter's summation included his own theory for the murderer's motive. He told the jury that he'd heard from the 'sub-curator of the Pathological Museum' at one of 'our great medical schools' information that might have a bearing on the inquiry. Months previously an American approached the sub-curator and asked him to procure uteri for which he would pay £20 each. The American's reasons for this request were even more bizarre. He claimed to be producing a publication and wished to supply a preserved uterus with each copy. Baxter stated that another medical institution had received a similar request, and suggested that the murderer might be engaged in supplying these organs. This raised the spectres of Burke and Hare, and Baxter suggested that the police should focus their enquiries among those with the necessary anatomical expertise.

Meanwhile, the police investigations were exceptionally thorough. Swanson's report details that they pursued several lines of inquiry. Occupants of 29, Hanbury Street were interviewed and their rooms searched. Statements were taken from adjoining houses. All common lodging houses in the area were checked to see whether anyone acting suspiciously had entered that morning. Chapman's history was investigated, anyone who knew her interviewed and their movements at the times of Tabram's, Nichols' and Chapman's death checked. Details were circulated and attempts made to trace anyone who'd been reported as a possible suspect. Enquiries were made at public houses in the area and local prostitutes were interviewed. 'The combined result of these enquiries,' Swanson notes in his report to the Home Office on 19 October, 'did not supply the police with the slightest clue to the murderer.' However there were, as we shall see, no shortage of suspects.

Interlude

'No Englishman could have perpetrated such a horrible crime…'

Mob member, quoted in *East London Observer*,
9 September 1888

Immediately following Annie Chapman's murder, the streets of Whitechapel seemed to reflect the fear and anger felt by its inhabitants. At night, the area was virtually deserted and many prostitutes were believed to have fled to safer districts. Those who were out after dark were most often plain-clothed policemen, some of whom were disguised as women in an effort to flush out the killer. Enraged mobs also roamed the streets, often taking justice into their own hands. Walter Dew, a Detective Constable at the time, related how a violent criminal named 'Squibby' came close to being lynched. He'd thrown a brick at a policeman and, when the police gave chase, they found themselves joined by an angry crowd who believed that the police were chasing the murderer.

Following the press comments about 'Leather Apron', anti-Semitic feelings became more pronounced. An influx of Jewish immigrants in 1881 had been met with sympathy but the economic depression had led to increased competition for the few jobs there were and the customary attitude of 'Them' coming over here and taking 'Our' jobs was never

far from the surface. Representatives of the Jewish community sought to quell the anti-Jewish feeling. Letters were
sent to newspapers explaining that Hebrew beliefs involved
a complex abhorrence of spilling blood. On 15 September,
the Day of Atonement, the Chief Rabbi, Dr Hermann Adler
spoke with the same message in mind, pleading for religious
tolerance and asserting that no Hebrew could be capable of
such appalling crimes. Samuel Montagu's offer of £100
reward was made with the same goal in mind, as was the
assembly of the Mile End Vigilance Committee, many of
whose members were Jewish tradesmen. These efforts to
show that East End Jews were as concerned for the safety of
the community as anyone calmed the public to some degree,
but a fear of anti-Semitic riots continued to haunt the pro-
ceedings and certainly remained a possibility for Sir Charles
Warren, the Metropolitan Chief Police Commissioner.

Mrs Darrell's testimony that the man she'd seen talking to
Chapman was 'foreign-looking' didn't help matters.
However, when her testimony was given on 19 September,
the atmosphere in the East End had relaxed and locals, particularly prostitutes, were beginning to take to the night
streets again. Not everyone was terrified by the crimes. Some
even found ways to profit by them. Inhabitants of houses over-
looking the backyard of 29, Hanbury Street charged members
of the public a small entrance fee so that they could see the
crime scene. A waxworks' owner in Whitechapel Road
splashed red paint on three of his female dummies and exhib-
ited them as Tabram, Nichols and Chapman.

Perhaps the group that profited most from the crimes was
the press. The sales of newspapers to bloodthirsty members
of the public eager to hear the latest about the atrocities

boosted sales like nothing before, and extra print runs were needed to meet requirements. Journalists from the tabloid *Star* to the upmarket *Daily Telegraph* rose to the challenge. Even the usually sedate *Times* wasn't exempt. All were equally keen to make political currency out of the murders. Both radical and conservative papers used coverage to criticise the Home Secretary and Sir Charles Warren.

Sir Charles Warren, in turn, was highly critical of the behaviour of the press. He angrily denounced them to Matthews for trailing police officers on their enquiries and re-interviewing people once the police had finished their questions. The CID's policy of maintaining secrecy to protect the investigation caused journalists to resort to such tactics. Journalists flocked to Wynne Baxter's lengthy inquests which supplied them with many of the details they couldn't glean from the police, and claimed that fuller reports could only help the police investigation.

The press and the public were only too keen to offer their own theories to the police. Was the killer a religious maniac on a crusade to clean up the vice-ridden streets of Whitechapel? Were the attacks motivated by revenge, the killer having contracted a venereal disease from a prostitute? Maybe he was the member of some heathen sect, or a Jewish ritual slaughterman seeking out human sacrifices. On 13 September, *The Star* suggested photographing Chapman's eyes (there was a widely-held belief that the human retina retained the last image it saw). This was politely ignored, but the Home Secretary would later suggest the same idea to Sir Charles Warren during the investigation of the next Ripper victim, Elizabeth Stride. After Chapman's murder Dr L Forbes Winslow, self-described 'medical theorist and practical detective,' offered the first of his suggestions to *The Times*, advising the police to check lunatic asylums for patients recently discharged or escaped. Winslow later became obsessed with the case to the degree that he patrolled the streets in search of clues.

Wynne Baxter's theory of the cash-hungry uterus collector was welcomed by the press but disputed by the medical fraternity. Most medical schools denied receiving such a request. University College and Middlesex Hospitals refused to confirm or deny the suggestion. Instead, their comments that the interests of justice were endangered by the disclosure suggest that they might have been approached by just such a journal publisher. By 6 October, the *British Medical Journal* sought to kill off the idea. They referred to a foreign physician of 'highest reputability' who had enquired eighteen months previously about securing certain anatomical specimens for scientific investigation. Their theory was that this request had been misinterpreted by 'a minor official'. No more was heard from Baxter on the subject.

Some Contemporary Suspects

At 7am on the morning of Annie Chapman's murder, Mrs Fiddymont, landlady of the Prince Albert pub in Brushfield Street (about 400 yards from 29, Hanbury Street) was in the bar with her friend Mary Chappell. While they were talking a rough-looking man came in and asked for ale. He looked 'so startling and terrifying' that their suspicions were immediately aroused. His shirt was torn on the right shoulder and a narrow streak of blood visible under his right ear. On the back of his right hand were several spots of blood and there was dried blood between his fingers. Seeing he was being watched, he drank up and left.

He was followed from the pub by Joseph Taylor, a builder, alerted by Mrs Fiddymont. Taylor followed the man as far as Half Moon Street, Bishopsgate. He described the man as middle-aged, medium height with short, sandy hair and a ginger moustache which curled at its ends. He had faint hollows under his cheekbones and his eyes were wild and staring. The man's dress was 'shabby-genteel', with pepper-and-salt trousers and a dark coat. When Taylor drew level with him to get a better look, 'his look was enough to frighten any woman'. The description would preoccupy Abberline during the arrest of several suspects. Two days after Annie Chapman's murder, the police thought they'd finally caught their man.

Leather Apron

On the morning of 10 September, Sergeant William Thick and another officer knocked at the door of 22, Mulberry Street. The door was opened by John Pizer, alias 'Leather Apron'. Allegedly Thick said: 'You are just the man I'm looking for.' Thick took Pizer to Leman Street Police station together with some knives found on the premises. This was so casually handled that they were inside the station before word spread that 'Leather Apron' had been captured and a huge crowd gathered outside. Inside, Pizer was interrogated about his movements on the nights of Nichols' and Chapman's murders. On the night of Nichols' death he was, he claimed, lodging at 'The Round-House' in Holloway Road. From 6 September, he had been in hiding at 22, Mulberry Street in fear for his life.

The police were able to verify these claims. The landlord of the Holloway Road lodging house remembered Pizer because, that night, there had been a fire at the Albert Docks. Seeing reflections of it in the sky, Pizer had discussed the fire with the landlord and two police officers outside. His brother told how Pizer had fled to lodgings in Westminster on 2 September after being pointed out as 'Leather Apron' and pursued by a 'howling crowd'. The Thursday before Chapman's death, Pizer had returned to Whitechapel. He had immediately gone into hiding at 22, Mulberry Street (his brother's and stepmother's home) on being told there was still 'false suspicion' of him.

Pizer was part of an identity parade held on 10 September. Mrs Fiddymont was unable to identify him but one Emmanuel Violenia claimed to have seen him threatening a woman with a knife in Hanbury Street the night Chapman died. Violenia added that he knew Pizer as 'Leather Apron'. Under further questioning Violenia was discredited. The police believed that he'd fabricated the story in order to see Chapman's body. Pizer was released.

On 12 September, Pizer was summoned to formally clear himself of suspicion of murder. His claim that Sergeant Thick had known him for eighteen years was cut short by the coroner. Thick, however, stated the same day that when people referred to 'Leather Apron', they meant Pizer (despite claims of Pizer, his friends and family to the contrary).

While Pizer was undoubtedly the 'John Pozer' sentenced to six months hard labour in July 1887 for attacking James Willis, a fellow boot-finisher, he was no longer under suspicion of being the Whitechapel murderer. On 11 October 1888, he successfully sued Emily Patswold for calling him 'Old Leather Apron' and attacking him. She was fined 10 shillings.

William Henry Pigott

53-year-old Pigott was arrested at Gravesend where he had attracted suspicion by loudly expressing a hatred of women. One of his hands was also injured. Sources alternately claim he was a ship's cook or a failed Hoxton publican. Both state that he was believed to be mentally unstable. He was arrested on 9 September in the Pope's Head Tavern. A paper parcel that he had left behind in a fish shop was found to contain clothing, including a bloodstained shirt with a torn pocket. Pigott claimed that he'd seen a woman collapse in a fit in Whitechapel about 4.30am on Saturday 8th. When he went to help her she bit his hand and he struck her in return. Seeing policemen heading towards him, he fled.

Informed by telegram of Pigott's arrest, Inspector Abberline escorted him back to Whitechapel where he was put in an identity parade. Neither Mrs Fiddymont nor Joseph Taylor picked him out. Mrs Chappell did so but remained uncertain about whether Pigott was indeed the man. The police found no evidence to connect Pigott to Chapman's death and his movements were accounted for. On 10 September, he was committed to the Whitechapel Workhouse Infirmary where he was treated for *delirium tremens* and later discharged.

Jacob Isenschmid

Isenschmid was a Swiss butcher, located in Holloway. When

his business failed, he suffered a nervous breakdown result-ing in a ten-week stay at Colney Hatch Asylum in 1887. On 11 September, acting on a letter from Doctors Cowan and Crabb of Holloway, who believed him to be the Whitechapel murderer, the police investigated his lodgings at 60, Milford Road and his former home at 97, Duncombe Road, Holloway, where his wife still lived. She told the police that she hadn't seen him in two months and that he often carried butchers' knives with him. His landlord reported that on the night of Annie Chapman's murder he'd come back at about 9pm and left again at 1am. He'd repeated the same pattern four times out of five previous nights. The police staked out both addresses until it was discovered that Isenschmid had been leaving at night to buy sheep's heads and other offcuts to dress and sell in the West End. By the later murders he was back in Colney Hatch.

Charles Ludwig (aka Charles Ludwig Wetzel)

Early in the morning of 18 September, prostitute Elizabeth Burns accompanied Charles Ludwig to Three Kings Court, The Minories, a small dark court near some railway arches. Here, Ludwig pulled a knife on her. Her cries of 'Murder!' attracted the attention of City PC John Johnson. Johnson sent Ludwig on his way and Burns went with the policeman. Obviously frightened, it was only then that she mentioned that Ludwig had threatened her with a knife. Johnson returned to the court, but Ludwig had vanished.

Ludwig resurfaced, the worse for drink, at about 3am at a coffee stall on Whitechapel High Street. Here he threat-ened Alexander Finlay with a long-bladed penknife. This drew the attention of PC John Gallagher who hauled him off to Leman Street police station. When searched he was found to be carrying a razor and a pair of long-bladed scissors. Brought before Thames Magistrates Court that day, he was charged with being drunk and disorderly and threatening to stab. The magistrate remanded him in custody for a week. During this time, the police laboured to find out everything that they could about him.

A recent immigrant, Ludwig had been employed as a barber's assistant by a Mr Partridge at Richter's, a German club in Houndsditch. Ludwig slept on the shop's floor for a while but then went to stay with a tailor named Johannes, in Church Street. Johannes apparently took exception to Ludwig's habits and forced him to leave on 17 September. That day, increasingly drunk, he went to Richter's and to a hotel in Finsbury where his threatening behaviour (he pulled razors on several people) caused him to be ejected. Partridge stood by him, after a fashion, claiming that Ludwig was too much of a coward to be the Whitechapel murderer. The landlord of the hotel was less supportive, stating that Ludwig had talked about the murders and was always in a bad temper, grinding his teeth with rage at any little thing that upset him. He further claimed Ludwig had also been a doctor's assistant in the army, where he had helped to dissect bodies, and often consorted with prostitutes.

The evidence against Ludwig made him appear a prime suspect. He was subjected to further periods of remand until his whereabouts during the previous weeks were investigated. He was finally released on 2 October. However, while he was in jail, his innocence was proved when the real murderer struck again...

Double Event

'We're all up to no good, and no one cares what becomes of us.'

Unidentified prostitute quoted by Dr Thomas
Barnardo, letter to The Times, October 6th 1888

Three weeks after Annie Chapman's murder, the police's best efforts had uncovered no suspects who proved to be the murderer and Whitechapel nightlife slowly returned to normal. The press still featured the murders prominently, fuelled with information from the lengthy Nichols and Chapman inquests. The murder of a woman near Gateshead on 22 September led many to believe the killer had fled to pastures new. The weekend of Saturday 29 September changed all that.

A Ripper Writes…

Just as there had been people claiming to have committed the murders wasting the police's time, there had also been letters admitting to the same, but on 27 September a letter arrived that demanded more attention. It was addressed simply to 'The Boss, Central News Office, London City' and postmarked September 27th, London EC, the same day that it was received at the Central News Agency at Ludgate Circus. It was written in red ink in an educated hand and ran:

25 Sept: 1888

Dear Boss

I keep on hearing the police have caught me but they wont fix me just yet. I have laughed when they look so clever and talk about being on the <u>right</u> track. That joke about Leather Apron gave me real fits. I am down on whores and I shant quit ripping them till I do get buckled. Grand work the last job was. I gave the lady no time to squeal. How can they catch me now. I love my work and want to start again. You will soon hear of me with my funny little games. I saved some of the proper <u>red</u> stuff in a ginger beer bottle over the last job to write with but it went thick like glue and I cant use it. Red ink is fit enough I hope <u>ha ha</u>. The next job I do I shall clip the ladys ears off and send to the police officers just for jolly wouldnt you. Keep this letter back till I do a bit more work, then give it out straight. My knife's so nice and sharp I want to get to work right away if I get a chance. Good luck.

Yours truly

Jack the Ripper

Dont mind me giving the trade name

A second postscript in red crayon was written at a right angle to the rest. It read:

wasnt good enough to post this before I got all the red ink off my hands curse it. No luck yet. They say I'm a doctor now <u>ha ha</u>

Two days later it was forwarded to Chief Constable Williamson at Scotland Yard. An attached letter by journalist Thomas Bulling explained that it 'was treated like a joke'. Whatever their first impression of the letter, the police certainly paid more notice to Jack's warning the next day.

Double Event

Dutfield's Yard sat on the west side of Berner Street (now Henriques Street), a southern turning off Commercial Road. The yard had been named after Arthur Dutfield, whose van and cart-making business had once been there. The large wooden gates at the yard's entrance still proclaimed Dutfield's connection, but now the yard housed only a sack warehouse and a disused stable. It was flanked on the left by a row of cottages. To its right stood the International Working Men's Educational Club, a Socialist meeting place mainly attended by Russian and Polish Jews. Entry to the club was either through the front door or by a side entrance past the gates in Dutfield's Yard. For this reason, the gates were usually left open. Any lighting in the yard came from the cottages or the club and only illuminated its top end. As a result, the first eighteen feet or so within the gates were pitch black after sunset.

On Saturday nights the club held free discussions. On Saturday 29 September, this had ended around midnight after which many of the ninety or so attendees had gone home.

Thirty-odd remained behind to socialise, sing and chat with their fellows. Although there was noise coming from the upstairs rooms of the club, it was not rowdy. Witnesses were certain that had there been a cry of 'Murder!' from the yard, they would have heard it. Between 12.30 and 12.40am several people, including the club's chairman, Morris Eagle, would leave and/or enter via Dutfield's Yard. All of them would later state that the yard had been empty.

Twenty minutes later, the situation was much different. Louis Diemschütz, the club steward, lived on the premises with his wife. On Saturdays he sold cheap jewellery at Westow Hill market, Crystal Palace. This Saturday was no different, and he returned to the club at 1.00am, intending to unload his unsold merchandise before stabling his pony and barrow at George Yard. Driving into Dutfield's Yard, the pony suddenly shied over to the left-hand side of the passage. Looking down to his right, Diemschütz noticed something lying on the ground. At first he tried to feel what it was with his whip. Still uncertain, he jumped down and struck a match. Lying by the club wall was a woman. He ran inside and told several members of his discovery. Returning outside with a lighted candle, they saw blood on the ground. Immediately Diemschütz headed towards Fairclough Street in search of the police. Morris Eagle also went for assistance, running toward Commercial Street. Diemschütz found no officer, but was followed back by Edward Spooner, a horse-keeper attracted by all the excitement. At the yard, someone lit a match and Spooner inspected the woman. He lifted her chin. It was still warm and blood still flowed from a deep cut in the throat.

Five minutes later, Morris Eagle returned with PC Henry Lamb and a fellow officer. Lamb was quick to get people to stand back from the body, lest they get blood on their clothes. Examining the woman, he noticed the blood that flowed towards the side door of the club had not yet congealed. He sent the other officer to fetch a doctor and Eagle to Leman Street police station for assistance.

Dr Frederick Blackwell arrived at the scene at about 1.16am and examined the body. By now the blood on the pavement had begun to dry. His findings on this brief examination included the following: Her legs were drawn up with her feet against the right side of the passage. Her neck, chest, legs and face were all slightly warm but her hands were cold. Her right hand was open, lying on her chest and smeared on both sides with blood. Her left hand, partially closed, contained a small packet of cachous (small aromatic sweetmeats sucked to sweeten the breath). Her face was quite placid. Around her neck was a check silk scarf, the bow of which was turned to the left and pulled tightly, suggesting that the murderer had pulled her back by it. There was a long incision in the neck, made from left to right. It had severed the vessels on the left side but not on the right, and had cut the windpipe completely in two. Blackwell noted that there were no spots of blood nearby nor on the clothing. He placed the time of death between twenty minutes and half an hour before he had arrived. She would have bled to death quite slowly but have been unable to cry out due to the severing of the windpipe. The injuries, he noted, were 'beyond self-infliction'.

After about half an hour Blackwell was joined by Dr Bagster Phillips who confirmed most of his findings. Phillips, however, stated that the woman had been alive 'within an hour' of his arrival. Their estimates, therefore, put the time of the murder as early as 12.36am or as late as 12.56am.

Meanwhile, PC Lamb had secured the gates and made pre-liminary searches of the club, the yard and the surrounding cottages. Those attending the club were held until their state-ments had been taken and their persons searched. Dr Phillips examined them for bloodstains. The body was removed to St George's Mortuary in Cable Street. By 5.30am, the last signs of the murder were washed away by PC Albert Collins. But by then events had moved on. The Ripper, it seemed, had not tired of his 'funny little games' for the night.

Approximately three-quarters of a mile and twelve min-utes walk away from Berner Street lay Mitre Square. It was situated just behind Mitre Street and was mainly enclosed by warehouses. A small, cobbled area of about twenty-four square yards, it was heavily trafficked by day but at night it was poorly lit and deserted. The lighting, such as it was in the square, meant that the south-west corner, by a row of deserted houses, was the darkest part. The solitude it offered made it a favoured haunt for prostitutes and their customers.

At about 1.44am, PC Edward Watkins of the City Police (Mitre Square lay just within the eastern boundary of City jurisdiction) completed his fifteen-minute circuit and arrived back in Mitre Square. When he had last walked through it, it had been deserted. This time, there were signs that it had been occupied during his absence. In that darkest corner was the body of a woman, her throat cut and her stomach ripped open, lying on her back in a pool of blood.

Within twenty minutes, Mitre Square was buzzing with police activity. Also summoned were Dr George Sequeira, who declared the woman dead, and police surgeon F Gordon Brown. Close to the body was found a mustard tin contain-ing two pawn tickets that would later aid identification. The body was taken to the City Mortuary at Golden Lane where Dr Brown, observed by Drs Sequeira, Sedgwick Saunders and Bagster Phillips, would perform the post-mortem.

Goulston Street Graffito

PC Alfred Long was one of the police drafted in from A Division (Westminster) during the night of the 'double event.' His second patrol of Goulston Street, at 2.55am, was a momentous one, for it revealed the first clue ever left by the Ripper in his flight back to Whitechapel and another clue that, whether left by the Ripper or not, proved to be one of the most controversial pieces of evidence discovered during the 'Autumn of Terror'. Outside the entrance to the staircase of Nos. 108–119, Wentworth Model Dwellings he found a piece of a woman's apron, still wet with blood. The piece would later be found to match a gap in Catharine Eddowes' apron exactly. There were no other traces of blood on the pavement nor on the stairwell, but on the right-hand side of the doorway to the dwellings' entrance there was a message, written in white chalk on the black bricks.

The message read, as best we can gather from notes taken at the time:

> The Juwes are
> The men That
> Will not
> be Blamed
> for nothing

Long took down the message. Arriving later, DC Daniel

Halse took down a version with a slightly different intention: 'The Juwes are not The men that Will be Blamed for nothing.' Other versions claim that the word was spelled 'Jewes' or 'Juews.'

Unfortunately, for the following reasons, these transcripts are all that we can rely on now.

Long took the apron to Commercial Street police station at around 3.05am. Following his alert both the City and the Metropolitan Police, including Halse, converged on Goulston Street. Notice was sent to Mitre Square where Inspector McWilliam ordered the message to be photographed and the surrounding tenements searched. The searches revealed no one who was likely to be the Ripper.

Sir Charles Warren was alerted to the situation and met with Superintendent Thomas Arnold at Leman Street. Here Arnold proposed that the writing be removed and had already dispatched an inspector with a sponge to await Warren's arrival before proceeding. Arnold's reasons are understandable but his methods remain questionable. The graffito was in a predominantly Jewish area, one which would soon be heavily populated by market traffic for Petticoat Lane. DC Halse protested at the erasure and suggested that the top line only should be erased. Another suggestion, that it be covered with a cloth was also vetoed. Under Warren's supervision (it has been rumoured, but never proven, that Warren erased the message himself) the message was removed. Twenty-two years later, the decision would still rankle. In his memoirs, Major Smith, acting City Police Commissioner, would refer to the erasure as an 'unpardonable blunder'.

Much discussion has surrounded the graffito. The main points are:

- That the killer threw the apron down by the message, which was already in place – which is fortuitous, but not impossible. Inspector Swanson notes that the writing looked blurred which suggests age (or possibly left-handedness, which the Ripper had not displayed), although others would state that it looked recent.
- The murderer must have written it, because an overtly anti-Semitic message written in such an area would soon have been obliterated by the inhabitants.
- Several newspapers, including the *Pall Mall Gazette*, erroneously stated that 'Juwes' is Yiddish for Jews, thereby suggesting that the killer was Jewish. Warren discussed this with the acting Chief Rabbi, who said that the Yiddish for Jews is 'Yidden'. Warren would earn the Rabbi's thanks for his actions in quelling further anti-Semitic protests.
- The murderer used deliberate subterfuge to incriminate the Jews and throw the police off the track. As we shall see, certain witness testimony suggests this theory is correct, if the Ripper was the murderer of...

Elizabeth Stride

Presided over by Wynne Baxter, the inquest into Elizabeth Stride's death was held at the Vestry Hall, Cable Street. It was as detailed and lengthy (reconvened 2, 5 and 23 October) as Catharine Eddowes' inquest would be expeditious. It was, at first, a confused affair, due to the fabrications that Stride had spun about her life and to Mrs Mary Malcolm who identified the body on 1 October as her sister, Mrs Elizabeth Watts. Malcolm claimed that every Saturday she met her sister on the corner of Chancery Lane to give her two shillings for her lodgings. That week she had had a premonition that something had happened to her sister and that Saturday she had waited in vain. On enquiring about the murder, the police had directed her to St George's Mortuary. It took her three sightings to finally confirm that the deceased was Mrs Watts. Much time was wasted with Mrs Malcolm, whose increasingly bizarre claims about her sister's behaviour were finally repudiated with the emergence of Mrs Watts, very much alive and not a little put out by Mrs Malcolm's stories. Stride was eventually identified beyond all doubt by PC Walter Stride, a nephew of her estranged husband, who had recognised her from a photograph.

Stride was born Elizabeth Gustafsdotter in 1843, in Torslanda near Gothenburg, Sweden. From 1860 she had worked as a domestic servant in Carl Johan parish, Gothenburg, before moving to Cathedral parish in 1862, again working as a domestic servant. In 1865, she had been registered as a prostitute and gave birth to a stillborn daughter. During this time she was twice admitted to hospital with venereal disease.

In 1866, she moved to London where, according to acquaintances, she had worked as a domestic for a gentleman living near Hyde Park. In 1869, she married John Stride at St Giles-in-the-Fields. Her marriage certificate gave her maiden name as Gustifson. During their marriage, they allegedly ran a coffee shop in Poplar and in March 1877 she was briefly admitted to Poplar Workhouse. It seems that their marriage had broken down by 1882. Elizabeth Tanner, deputy keeper of a common lodging house at 32, Flower and Dean Street testified that Stride had lived there on and off since that year. It was there that she gained the nickname 'Long Liz' (not because of her height, 5 feet 5 inches, but because it is a common East End epithet for people named Stride).

Stride always told friends that she had lost her husband and two children in 1878, when they had drowned, along with 600 other passengers on the *Princess Alice*. The leisure steamer had collided with the collier *Bywell Castle* on the Thames, near Woolwich. Her story was untrue. John Stride did not die until 1884 (in Bromley, of heart disease) and they had no children.

By 1885 she was living with Michael Kidney, a waterside labourer, either at 38, Dorset Street or 36, Devonshire Street, Commercial Road (again, accounts differ). The latter's proximity to the docks seems the more credible. They supported themselves on Kidney's earnings and Stride's domestic work. Kidney testified that, during their three years together, she'd been away from him for about five months in total. He blamed her liking for drink. Between 1887 and 1888 she had been convicted eight times for drunkenness. But this is probably not the whole truth. There is no doubt that they quarrelled, and Kidney does not seem to have been as mild-mannered as he presented himself at the inquest. In April 1887, Stride had him charged with assault but then she failed to appear in court to prosecute him. It seems likely that, after quarrels, she would leave to avoid further assaults.

Kidney claimed that he had last seen her in Commercial Street on 25 September and was surprised that she was not home when he returned from work that evening. She probably returned to 32, Flower and Dean Street, and was certainly there on 26 September. This verification comes from a surprising source – Dr Thomas Barnardo. He had been talking to the residents of 32 on Wednesday evening, eliciting responses for his proposals to save the children of prostitutes from the streets. He had occasion to view the remains of 'Long Liz' and recognised her immediately as one of the women that he had seen in the kitchen of the lodging house that evening. The same day, Stride had returned home to remove some personal belongings, another sign that they had quarrelled recently and she planned to stay out of Kidney's way for some time. Stride was only an occasional prostitute, relying more on money from Kidney and charring work. Elizabeth Tanner recalled being told that she 'was at work among the Jews', and on 29 September Stride cleaned two of the lodging rooms, for which Tanner paid her sixpence. Tanner last saw her when they met for a drink at 6.30 that evening at the Queen's Head, Commercial Street and walked back to the lodging house together.

It is known that Stride left again after 7.00pm but there are no other sightings of her until around 11.00pm when Mr J Best and John Gardner saw her leave the Bricklayer's Arms in Settle Street in the company of a young Englishman of 'clerkly' appearance. He had a black moustache and wore a morning suit and a billycock hat. They headed in the direction of Commercial Road and Berner Street. Forty-five minutes later, William Marshall saw her with an Englishman on Berner Street heading toward Dutfield's Yard. The man he described was similar to Best and Gardner's descriptions. Supposedly he overheard the man say: 'You would say anything but your prayers.'

PC William Smith saw the couple at the same place at

12.35am. He noticed that the woman had a red rose on her coat and would later identify the body as that same woman. He described the man as 28, 5 feet 7 inches tall, with a dark complexion and a small dark moustache. He was wearing a black diagonal coat, a hard felt deerstalker hat and a white collar and tie. In one hand he was carrying a parcel wrapped in newspaper. Both appeared to be sober. Smith heard none of their conversation.

More important is the testimony of Israel Schwartz, a Hungarian Jew who lived in Ellen Street (which crossed Berner Street). Inspector Swanson's report to the Home Office on 19 October is the only record of this testimony, given at Leman Street police station on 30 September. Schwartz had got as far as the gateway to Dutfield's Yard when he saw a man stop and speak to a woman stood in the gateway. The man tried to pull her into the street but turned her round and threw her down. She screamed three times but not very loudly. Schwartz crossed to the opposite side of the street. As he did so he saw a second man lighting his pipe. The man with the woman called out (apparently to the man on the opposite side of the road), 'Lipski'. Schwartz walked away but, finding that the second man was following him, ran as far as the railway arch. By then the other man had stopped.

Schwartz did not know whether the two men knew each other but felt that, because of this exchange, they did. He described the first man as about 30, 5 feet 5 inches tall, of fair complexion with dark hair and a small brown moustache. He was full faced and broad shouldered with a dark jacket and trousers, wearing a black, peaked cap. The second man was taller, about 5 feet 11 inches, and about 35 years old. His hair and moustache were light brown. He wore a dark overcoat and an old black hard felt hat with a wide brim. Given that Stride was dead fifteen minutes later, Schwartz's report was widely accepted by the police as being a glimpse of the killer. The phrase used by the man was much discussed by the police. Swanson felt that 'Lipski' implied that the killer was Jewish. This was read the same way by the Home Office, who assumed that he was addressing the second man as 'Lipski', implying that, not only was the killer a Jew, but also that he had a Jewish accomplice.

Inspector Abberline, with his knowledge of the area, reversed this theory entirely. He pointed out that the previous year Israel Lipski had been hanged for the murder of a Jewish woman. Since then, his surname had been used as an insulting epithet to Jews in the East End. Other possibilities suggested are that the man used it as a verb (i.e. 'I am going to "Lipski" this woman' – although, as Lipski actually used poison, this seems a little tenuous) or, as Philip Sugden suggests, it was used to disguise the identity of the second man and, as with the Goulston Street graffito, to imply that Jews were behind the Whitechapel murders.

Despite the seeming importance of Schwartz's evidence there is no record of him ever testifying at Stride's inquest. Although all of Baxter's inquest papers into the Ripper's victims are missing, no press reports carry Schwartz's testimony. One of Dr Robert Anderson's memos during the police debate over the meaning of 'Lipski' mentions that he did testify. If this wasn't an error on Anderson's part then it suggests that the newspapers withheld reporting his evidence on the grounds that it might, once more, inflame anti-Semitic feeling. Wynne Baxter was notably thorough in hearing all evidence and the police would certainly have been acting unlawfully to have kept Schwartz from attending. Given the haste to erase the Goulston Street graffito, this wouldn't be entirely out of the question.

The statement of Mrs Fanny Mortimer, through inaccurate reporting, brings us the most enduring Ripper myth. In her statement, she mentions 'the only man whom I had seen pass through the street previously was a young man carrying a black shiny bag, who walked very fast down the street from Commercial Road'. The man, Leon Goldstein, voluntarily reported to Leman Street police station to clear himself. His bag contained empty cigarette boxes. However, connected with Bagster Phillips' speculation that the killer might be a doctor, the black bag fixed itself in the public consciousness and has remained there ever since.

Elizabeth Stride's post-mortem was conducted at St George's Mortuary by both Dr Blackwell and Dr Phillips. Phillips noted that the throat wound bore signs of having been inflicted by a short, probably blunt, blade, like a shoemaker's knife. No other injuries were found. There was some bluish discoloration to both shoulders, pressure marks, which suggested that Stride had been forced to the ground. Her left ear lobe had been torn at some previous juncture, but had long since healed over. Phillips found no trace of narcotics or anaesthetic in her stomach.

The post-mortem did raise one or two interesting differences between this and the previous murders which even now leave Elizabeth Stride's inclusion as a Ripper murder debatable but irresolvable. There were no abdominal mutilations (although the arrival of Diemschütz and his carriage probably interfered with the Ripper's plans). There was no evidence that Stride had been strangled prior to having her throat cut. Plus, if Schwartz did see Stride's killer, his aggressive and vocal behaviour seems to bear no relation to the silent, solitary murderer of Nichols and Chapman. However, like Nichols and Chapman, it appeared that the killer cut Stride's throat while she was down on her back. Lack of evidence of a struggle suggests that she was unconscious before the fatal knife strokes. This brings us back to the possibility that it was the Ripper who killed her and only the arrival of Louis Diemschütz dissuaded him from continuing his work on Elizabeth Stride.

It has been argued that Stride was murdered by Michael Kidney, that Schwartz witnessed the start of it and that the third man was possibly Stride's lover, who fled rather than be exposed by the investigation. Theorists' reasoning rests on Kidney's violent nature and his drunken appearance at Leman Street police station on 1 October, accusing the police of being unable to catch Stride's killer. At that point, the police were supposedly still struggling to identify Stride, hindered by Mrs Malcolm, so (the theory goes) Kidney could have only known of her death by committing it. However, *The Times'* coverage of the first day of the inquest (1 October), names the victim as Elizabeth Stride. It seems likely that, by the night of 1 October, when Kidney drunkenly upbraided the police, he could have known Stride was dead by sources other than first-hand experience. All the same…

Needless to say, the jury returned a verdict of 'Wilful murder by person or persons unknown'.

Catharine Eddowes

The Eddowes inquest, which opened on 4 October, was reconvened and concluded exactly a week later. It was presided over by the City Coroner, Mr Samuel Langham at the Golden Lane Mortuary. In one of several boundary disputes, protests were raised that Wynne Baxter should preside over the inquest as he had over the others. Langham would have none of this, stating that, as the body had been brought to a City mortuary, it was up to the City of London to hold the inquest. The brevity of the inquest aside (compared to those presided over by Baxter), witness testimony still helps us piece together Eddowes' life and last movements before she fell to the Ripper.

Catharine Eddowes was born in 1842 in Wolverhampton. She was the fifth of eleven children born to George and Catharine Eddowes. George worked in the then-prosperous tin plate industry. Despite this, the family moved to London, settling in Bermondsey. In 1855, tragedy struck when Catharine senior died of phthisis. The family then dispersed. Catharine, or Kate as she was to be known in later life, was sent to live with an aunt in Wolverhampton. She ran away to Birmingham after supposedly robbing her employer. There she briefly lived with an uncle before falling in love, at the age of sixteen, with Thomas Conway. Little is known about him, although he was apparently drawing a pension from the 18th Royal Irish Regiment. During the time they lived together as a common-law couple, he worked as a hawker. They had three children, Annie (1865), George (1868) and another son in 1873. Conway also tattooed his initials 'T C' on

Kate's left forearm. Friends from this time remembered her as an intelligent woman with a fiery temper.

In 1880, the couple separated. As usual, different parties gave different reasons. Annie blamed Kate's habitual drinking and absences. Kate's sister, Elizabeth, attributed the split to Conway's drinking and violent behaviour. By 1881, Kate was back in London and living with an Irish porter, John Kelly, at Cooney's Lodging House, 55, Flower and Dean Street. During this time, she went under the name of Kate Conway. The time that they were together seems to have been happy but poverty-stricken. Kate was known by most of her acquaintances as being 'a regular jolly sort' and if she and Kelly quarrelled it was rare and usually the result of drink.

In 1885, Annie, her daughter, married and spent the next couple of years moving around London, generally to avoid her mother's unannounced visits to scrounge money. However, most of Kate's friends, along with Kelly and Frederick Wilkinson, deputy keeper of Cooney's, were quick to state that Kate was not a prostitute and she mainly subsisted by charring and hawking. Probably she did solicit occasionally to earn money but Kelly and Wilkinson wouldn't have testified otherwise for fear of being charged with living off immoral earnings or running a disorderly house.

In September 1888, Kate and Kelly went hop picking in Kent. They returned at the end of the month, after an unsuccessful time. During their journey they met up with Emily Birrell and her man. Birrell gave Kate a pawn ticket for a shirt, which she thought would fit Kelly. They arrived back in London on 27 September, where they spent the night in the casual ward at Shoe Lane. Next morning, realising they had no money for lodgings, Kate went to spend the night at

Mile End casual ward, entreating Kelly to use what money they had for a bed at Cooney's.

They met again the next morning (Saturday 29 September). Kelly insisted on pawning a pair of his boots for 2/6 in order to buy food. This they ate in the kitchen at Cooney's. It is likely that they also bought liquor for, broke once more, Kate left at 2.00pm to go to Bermondsey to borrow money from Anne. Kelly recalled begging her to return home early, reminding her of the murders. Kate's last words to him were: 'Don't you fear for me. I'll take care of myself and I shan't fall into his hands.' She didn't go to see her daughter. The visit would have been pointless anyway, as Anne had moved from the address at least a year before. At the time of Kate's death, she was living in Southwark.

It is not clear where she got money from but at 8.30pm Kate was arrested for being drunk and disorderly in Aldgate High Street (Tom Cullen reports that she was impersonating a fire engine). It took two police officers to get her to Bishopsgate Police station. Here she gave her name as 'Nothing' and was locked in a cell. By 8.50pm she was asleep. PC George Hutt came on duty at 9.45pm and checked in on her at regular intervals during the night. By 12.15am she was awake and singing quietly to herself. At 12.30am she began to ask Hutt what time she would be released. He did so at about 1.00am when he was sure that she was sober enough.

Leaving, she gave her name as Mary Ann Kelly of 6 Fashion Street. It is this name that led Stephen Knight (in *Jack The Ripper: The Final Solution*) to suggest that Kate was not the Ripper's intended victim but that the killer was misled by this alias. However, it is not stated how the Ripper would have got hold of this information, if he had known where to look for it. Hutt guided her out, asking her to close the outer door behind her. Kate's last recorded words are: 'All right. Good night, old cock.'

Joseph Lawende, Joseph Hiram Levy and Harry Harris left the Imperial Club in Duke Street around 1.35am. They saw a man and a woman facing each other at the corner of Church Passage, leading into Mitre Square. They were talking quietly, the woman with her hand on the man's chest. Levy noticed that the man was about three inches taller than the woman but would later be unable to describe the couple further. Lawende saw more, being closer. The woman, he said, was wearing a black jacket and bonnet. The man he described as being about 30, 5 feet 7 inches tall, with a fair complexion and moustache. He was of medium build and wore a pepper-and-salt loose jacket and a peaked, grey cloth cap. Around his neck he wore a reddish neckerchief tied in a knot. He had the appearance of a sailor. Lawende doubted that he would be able to identify him again. Although he was unable to describe the woman, he identified Kate at the mortuary by her clothing. That Eddowes was found dead nine minutes later a few yards away, makes it likely she was Lawende's woman. His description of the man also tallies closely with those of Schwartz's, Marshall's and Smith's.

Dr Brown's findings from the crime scene and autopsy are conflated here. From the site he noted that the body was still warm and had been there for half an hour at the most. He believed that death was caused by the throat being cut, opening the left carotid artery. Her throat was then cut from left to right, severing the larynx and neck down to the vertebrae. The abdomen had been laid open from the breast bone to the pubes by an upwards jagged incision. The liver had been slit with separate incisions. The intestines had been drawn out and placed over the right shoulder, one piece of about two feet had been severed completely and placed between the body and the left arm, apparently by design. The right ear lobe and auricle had been cut through. Further cuts were made, opening the abdomen, extending across the thighs and labia and across over the liver. The pancreas and spleen had also been cut. The left kidney had been carefully taken out and removed. (Brown notes: 'I should say that someone who knew the position of the kidney must have done it.') The lining membrane over the uterus was cut through and the womb cut through horizontally, leaving a stump of 3/4 inch – the rest had been taken away. Brown would further note that the removal of the noted organs would be 'of no use for any professional purpose'.

Eddowes was the first victim to suffer facial mutilation. The left and right eyelid sustained cuts. There was a deep cut to the bone from the bridge of the nose down to the right cheek at the jawline. The tip of the nose had been detached by a cut that also divided the upper lip. There were other cuts at the top of the nose, at the right angle of the mouth and to both cheeks raising triangular flaps of about 1.5 inches in area.

Brown concluded that the murder and mutilations must have taken place at the spot where the body was found. As with the cases of Nichols, Chapman and Stride, it was likely that the murderer had been on Eddowes' right-hand side to avoid the worst of the blood. Brown estimated the knife to have been at least six inches long and attributed to the killer both anatomical knowledge (the kidneys, being covered with membrane, could easily be overlooked by someone without such knowledge) and surgical skill. Brown did not believe the killer was a doctor. Of the others present at the post-mortem, both Sequeira and Saunders expressed uncertainty over whether the killer had sought out the kidney or discovered it by accident but both concurred with Brown that he possessed some skill with a knife. Phillips expressed similar beliefs but saw less expertise demonstrated on Eddowes than on Chapman and thus doubted that the murders had been committed by the same man.

More recent medical testimony from examining the photographs express doubt at the killer's surgical ability but, given the speed (he had approximately ten minutes) and surroundings (practically unlit with the constant fear of discovery) in which the killer performed his operation, it is still astounding that he managed half of what he achieved in mutilating Eddowes' body. Dr Brown's belief that only one person committed the murder led the inquest jury's verdict of 'Wilful murder by some person unknown'.

While the upper classes expressed their sympathies in the press for the two women with outraged calls for social reform, the East End did their best to show tribute in their final send-offs. Elizabeth Stride's funeral took place on 8 October. She was buried in a pauper's grave at East London cemetery. The funeral was sparsely attended. In contrast, Catharine Eddowes' funeral procession from Golden Lane to the City of London cemetery in Ilford saw crowds lining most of the streets along the way and the funeral paid for by the undertaker, Mr G Hawkes of Spitalfields. In attendance were John Kelly and four of Catharine's sisters. According to various sources, the procession was followed by a wagon holding many of Catharine's female acquaintances from Flower and Dean Street.

A Study in Terror

'…I try and frighten them and speak of the danger they
run (they just) laugh and say, "Oh, I know what you
mean. I ain't afraid of him. It's the Ripper or the bridge
with me. What's the odds?"

Chief Inspector Henry Moore

The day after the two murders, the Central News Agency
heard from their correspondent again. This time it was a
postcard, undated but seemingly bloodstained and in the
same handwriting. It was postmarked the day of its delivery,
October 1st, from London E. Written in red crayon, Jack
was in fine gloating form:

> I wasnt codding dear old Boss when I gave you the tip.
> youll hear about saucy Jackys work tomorrow double
> event this time number one squealed a bit couldnt
> finish straight off. had not time to get ears for police
> thanks for keeping last letter back till I got to work
> again.

Jack the Ripper

In attempts to draw fresh information from the public, the
police distributed the letters to the press and posted facsim-
iles outside every police station. As a result, they were del-

uged, not merely with information but with floods of crank letters, many claiming to be from Jack himself. The decline of 'Leather Apron' following Pizer's acquittal no longer mattered; the police, the press, businesses and even private individuals received letters that claimed to be from Jack. The police, fearing that passing up any one of them could cost them the lead they desperately needed, attempted to check the veracity of each letter and trace the writers, wasting many valuable man hours.

The provenance of the original letter and postcard is another area of the Ripper case that has provoked much discussion. It is likely that they are both hoaxes coming from the same source since the second apparently picks up the conversational threads of the first. Long after the Ripper scare was over both Robert Anderson and Donald Swanson wrote that the letters were the work of a journalist whom they knew.

Suggested authors include Thomas Bulling (although his handwriting differs considerably) and the unidentified Best. In 1931, Best admitted to a journalist that he was responsible for writing all the Ripper letters to 'keep the business alive'. Maybe, but he was probably unaware of the hundreds of letters that were received. Of the first two, the second appears to display too much knowledge not to be from the Ripper, especially as the letter was postmarked the day that the press reported the story. However, several late editions on the Sunday (30 September) carried reports of the 'double event.' Plus, the letter was posted in East London, where the writer would, in all likelihood, have had easy access to information on the victims' deaths because the press were already swarming around both murder sites for details from police and public alike.

From Hell

The one letter that may deserve more attention is the one received by George Lusk of the Mile End Vigilance Committee. It arrived in a small package bearing two penny stamps and an illegible postmark. Along with the letter was half a rotting kidney. The letter read:

From Hell

Mr Lusk
   Sor
     I send you half the Kidne I took from one women prasarved it for you tother piece I fried and ate it was very nise I may send you the bloody knif that took it out if you only wate a whil longer
   signed   Catch me when
         you can
      Mishter Lusk

The kidney was taken to Dr Frederick Wiles. He was not there, but his assistant, Mr Reed, was. His opinion was that it was a human kidney, preserved in spirits of wine. He took it to Dr Thomas Openshaw at London Hospital.

Openshaw's examination, according to Reed, revealed that it was part of a female's left kidney. Also, it was a 'ginny' kidney belonging to someone suffering from Bright's disease and that the person had died about the same time as the victim of the Mitre Square murder. The next day, Openshaw denied these claims. Dr Sedgwick Saunders pointed out that the age and sex of a kidney could only be determined if the body was present and that gin left no traces in the kidney. He further noted that Eddowes' remaining kidney had been perfectly healthy and thus its extracted companion should be equally healthy. Saunders considered the whole thing a medical student hoax.

However, following Openshaw's supposed verdict, Lusk's group took the parcel to Inspector Abberline. The Met sent it to the City branch where it was examined by Dr Gordon Brown. Brown's report has not survived and so all information about the kidney comes from surviving police reports. From these we learn that the kidney came from a human adult and that it was not charged with fluid (indicating that it had not been handed over to a hospital or medical school). The renal artery is about three inches long. Eddowes' corpse retained two inches and the kidney had one inch attached. The right kidney was, Brown's statement confirms, in the advanced stages of Bright's disease and the kidney that Lusk received was in a similar condition. Most notably, of the surgeons that Brown consulted with, Mr Sutton of London Hospital (an authority on the kidney and its diseases) swore on his career that the extracted kidney had been preserved in spirits within hours of its removal, thus making it explicit that it had been removed at the scene. Organs destined for dissection would have been preserved in formaldehyde. Bodies of those dying from violence would not be taken immediately to the dissecting room but would await an inquest, held the next day at the earliest. Wynne Baxter would add a note of conjecture by stating that spirits of wine were the standard preservative for dissecting rooms.

Of the letter, a Miss Emily Marsh of 218, Jubilee Street, Mile End Road came forward to state that on 15 October she was in her father's shop when a tall man dressed in clerical garb entered. Pointing to the vigilance committee reward poster in the window, he asked for Mr Lusk's address. Miss Marsh showed him a newspaper that gave the address as Alderney Road, near Globe Road, Mile End. She read it out at the man's insistence and he wrote it down. When he left, she asked the shop boy to follow him. They described the man as around forty-five years old, 6 feet tall and slimly built. He wore a soft felt black hat, a stand-up collar and a long black single-breasted overcoat with a Prussian or clerical collar turned up. His complexion was sallow and he had a dark beard and moustache. He spoke with an Irish accent.

It's likely that this was the man who posted the kidney, for the address on the parcel was exactly what he'd copied down, with no street number, and some of the words ('Sor' 'Mishter') suggest an Irish accent. But whether this was the Ripper is another matter entirely.

The Lusk letter has been accepted as authentic by many theorists but, like so many positive things attached to the case, it remains inconclusive. In 1974, Thomas Mann (sic), a qualified document examiner, examined the letter. From the writing style and the types of errors in the letter Mann declared the writer to be semi-literate, rather than an educated person disguising their writing characteristics. Despite such expert testimony, we can still only assume that the letter to Lusk was written by the Ripper. The evidence appears weighted in its favour but it is by no means conclusive.

The Met's investigation following Elizabeth Stride's death was exhaustive. Along with the distribution of the Ripper's two missives to the newspapers, 80,000 leaflets were delivered to households and lodging houses in the area, appealing for anyone with information to come forth. The police presence continued to be bolstered by men from other divisions. The police detained at least eighty suspects and were watching the movements of a further 300, all follow-ups to information received. House-to-house enquiries were made and in many cases the premises were searched. Donald Swanson reported to the Home Office on 19 October 1888 that over 2000 lodgers were examined during this period. Sailors were checked by the Thames Police. All Asiatics were checked after a suggestion from an Indian correspondent to *The Times* that the mutilations to Eddowes' face seemed 'peculiarly Eastern'. Following the perceived Americanisms in the Ripper letters (e.g. 'Boss', 'shan't quit') the police checked the whereabouts of any Americans in the East End, including three cowboys in town as part of an American Exhibition. In total, 76 butchers and slaughtermen were questioned as well as Greek gypsies. Following the misinterpretation of Mrs Mortimer's evidence, men with black bags were stopped and searched (and often chased by members of the public). One of the more bizarre suggestions posited German thieves using the stolen uteri to put their potential victims to sleep by occult means!

All suggestions and suspicions, however curious, were pursued. Swanson's report notes that there are '994 dockets besides police reports'. Inspector Abberline would often leave work and patrol Whitechapel until four or five in the morning before retiring for the night. On many occasions he would be summoned back immediately to Whitechapel to interview another suspect. Certainly, the Ripper case nearly broke him, and the pressure on most of the police force was not aided in other quarters. Their lack of success was con-tinually attacked by the press, who ridiculed Sir Charles Warren's failure to organise his men properly. Papers of all political stripes united in calling for Matthews' and Warren's resignations. While private rewards offered exceeded £1,200, Matthews continued to vacillate. Now aware that any change of heart would be viewed as an embarrassing climb-down, he sought to implicate the Commissioner by offering a reward only on Warren's admission of police defeat. Warren immediately saw through this and back-tracked. The stalemate continued.

Despite doubts about their being able to function properly within Whitechapel's heavily-populated streets, bloodhounds were also tested. Several successful trials of the two dogs, Barnaby and Burgho, were held in Regent's Park and Hyde Park in early October, with Sir Charles Warren twice playing the hunted man. The press and public supported their use, believing their introduction was keeping the Ripper at bay. Warren was clearly impressed enough to leave orders that, should another murder occur, nothing be touched until the dogs were brought to the scene. This order appears not to have been retracted and caused a long delay in investigating Mary Kelly's murder. By then, the bloodhounds' owner had reclaimed them, once it became clear that the police weren't prepared to buy them or pay for their upkeep.

Other, more worrying suggestions, were made. Sir John Whittaker Ellis, a former Lord Mayor of London, proposed the police draw a half-mile cordon around Whitechapel and search every house in that area. Warren resisted, wisely seeing that such an operation, as well as being illegal, had the very real possibility of causing rioting and further damaging

the police's reputation. In the end, the search area was confined to houses within Spitalfields and Whitechapel bounded
roughly by Whitechapel Road to the south, Dunk Street to
the east, Buxton Street and the Great Eastern Railway to the
north and halting to the west at the City boundary.
Properties were only searched with owners' consent, but
such was the response from people that they met with little
obstruction. Dr Robert Anderson noted a week later that
'the public generally and especially the inhabitants of the
East End have shown a marked desire to assist in every way,
even at some sacrifice to themselves, as for example in per-
mitting their houses to be searched'.

Anderson appears to have been little help. Appointed
Assistant Commissioner for Crime on the day of Polly
Nichols' murder, he went on extended sick leave to
Switzerland the day Annie Chapman was found. Hastily
recalled, following the double murder, and given personal
responsibility for the case by Warren and Matthews, his first
proposal was even more short-sighted than that of Ellis.
Taken aback by prostitutes having police protection, he suggested that any woman 'on the prowl' after midnight, should
be arrested immediately. Given that a conservative estimate
placed the number of prostitutes operating in Whitechapel
at 1,200, his suggestion was not only inoperable but incred-
ibly out of touch with the problems faced by women in the
area.

October wore on with no further atrocities. The
increased police presence and heightened public awareness
probably kept the Ripper from operating during this period.
With more legitimate trades, such as charring and hawking,
oversubscribed as always, prostitutes, driven by the need for

the basic necessities of food and lodgings, began to venture out after dark once more.

Mary Jane Kelly

One woman who certainly needed money that October was Mary Jane (or Marie Jeanette) Kelly. Like hundreds of others, she was already nervous about the Ripper. Her lover, Joseph Barnett, testified that she asked him to read out the latest newspaper reports on the case. But, Ripper or not, money was tight and she already owed 29 shillings in back rent. Her attempts to earn money on the night of 8 November would result in the most infamous of the Ripper's crimes, bringing his reign of terror to a horrific climax.

She was born in Limerick around 1863 and had six or seven brothers and one sister. In early childhood her family moved to Wales where John Kelly, her father, worked in an ironworks. Around 1879 she married a collier named Davies but was widowed two or three years later when he was killed in a pit explosion. She moved to London in 1884 and worked at a high-class West End brothel for a time. At the invitation of one of 'her gentlemen' she went to live in Paris but returned to London a fortnight later as she didn't like it. She then lived on Ratcliffe Highway before moving in with a man named Morganstone at Stepney. Later, she lived in Bethnal Green Road with a plasterer, Joseph Fleming. Kelly remained fond of him and he continued to visit her after they separated. Julia Venturney, who lived at 1, Miller's Court, remembered Fleming and testified that he had 'often ill-used her because she cohabited with Joe (Barnett)'.

Mary met Joseph Barnett in 1887 when she lived at Cooly's lodging house in Thrawl Street. Barnett, an Irish cockney, worked as a fish porter at Billingsgate. They first met in Commercial Street and had a drink together. Their friendship was immediate and, after a couple more encounters that same week, they decided to live together. They seem to have been well suited. By Barnett's testimony they lived together for a year and eight months. During this time they moved around the area taking lodgings in several addresses.

From the start of 1888, they finally settled at 13, Miller's Court. The couple rented the room, at 4/6 a week, from John McCarthy, who owned the chandler's shop at 27, Dorset Street. Miller's Court was one of several courts off Dorset Street and was accessible by a narrow passageway between numbers 26 and 27. The court was a small paved yard, flanked by run-down tenement houses, with a single gas lamp. Number 13 backed onto 26, Dorset Street and had originally been number 26's back-parlour before being partitioned off when the rest of the building had been let out as furnished rooms. (It now lies under a multi-storey car park in Dorset Street.)

During their time together, there is no account or inference that Barnett was violent and generally they did not drink excessively. Kelly did occasionally get drunk. Towards the end of their relationship she had broken one of the two windows in the room in a drunken temper. Their quarrels seem to have been rooted in Barnett's dislike of Kelly's prostitution. He regularly gave her money so that she would not have to walk the streets. Barnett's reason for their separation on 30 October was that Kelly was allowing another prostitute to share their room. At the inquest he admitted that he had been out of work, but denied that this had any bearing on their parting. He had been fired from his job at Billingsgate several months before (possibly for theft) and despite taking labouring jobs where he could, they soon fell behind with the rent. Kelly's return to prostitution cannot have helped their relationship.

Following their separation, Barnett moved into lodgings in Bishopsgate. Despite their differences they remained friends and Barnett continued to visit Kelly, giving her money when he could. Barnett testified that he visited her on the evening of 8 November to apologise because he couldn't give her any money as he had no work.

Barnett visited her between 7.30 and 7.45pm. Maria Harvey, who had been visiting, left at that point. It seems likely that Harvey was not the prostitute who caused Barnett to leave in the first place, but a second guest whom Kelly had invited to stay. Harvey had stayed on the Monday and Tuesday and had then moved to a room at 3, New Court, Dorset Street. Also present, according to a press interview, was Lizzie Albrook, a friend of Kelly's who lived in Miller's Court. She left after Barnett's arrival. Barnett's statement mentions only 'a woman,' so someone was lying. The next time we hear of Kelly, she is 'intoxicated'. At midnight, Mary Ann Cox, another prostitute, who lived at 5, Miller's Court, met Kelly at the entrance to the court. With Kelly was a short (about 5 feet 5 inches), stout man, wearing a longish, shabby, dark coat and a hard, black billycock hat. He had a blotchy face, full carroty moustache and a clean chin. Cox bade her good night and the couple went into number 13. Kelly was heard to start singing. Cox stated that she would know the man again. She left her own room again at 12.15am to look for customers. It was a bitter night and raining most of the time. When she returned at 1.00am to warm herself before setting out once more, Kelly was still singing.

The next witness to enter the scene is Elizabeth Prater from 20, Miller's Court, which was the room above Kelly's. From 1.00am she had been waiting outside 27, Dorset Street for the man that she lived with to appear. At 1.20am she gave up and went upstairs to her room. Through the partition she could see a glimmer of light but heard no singing nor sounds of movement. Nervous of the Ripper, she put two tables against the door and, slightly drunk, retired to bed.

Sarah Lewis was a laundress who lived at 29, Great Pearl Street. After 'words' with her husband, she went to stay with friends on the first floor room of 2, Miller's Court. She heard the clock of Christ Church, Spitalfields, strike 2.30am as she arrived. Standing alone in the doorway of a lodging house opposite the court was a man. She described him as 'not tall, but stout,' with a wide-awake black hat. She did not notice his clothes. He was looking up the court 'as if waiting for someone to come out'. Mary Cox returned home at 3.00am. The light was out at number 13 and she heard nothing the rest of the night.

Around 3.30am Sarah Lewis, who had been dozing in a chair, awoke. At about the same time, Elizabeth Prater was woken by her kitten climbing over her neck. Both of them testified that shortly afterwards they heard a woman cry 'Oh! Murder!' It was faint but seemingly nearby. Neither of them checked, however. Prater went back to sleep. Lewis stayed awake until five.

At 8.30 that morning, Caroline Maxwell, the wife of a lodging house deputy in Dorset Street, saw Mary Kelly outside Miller's Court. She testified that she had known her for four months but only spoken to her twice during that time. Maxwell asked Kelly why she was up so early, and was told she had the 'horrors of drink' upon her. Later, returning from Bishopsgate at around 8.45am she saw Kelly again outside the Britannia pub talking to a man. Although she only saw them from a distance she was certain that it was Kelly. The man was not tall, and wore dark clothes and a plaid coat.

Whether you accept Maxwell's testimony (which, given the coroner's estimate of time of death, means that it verges on the Fortean), depends on whose theory you are accepting. There are theories for all aspects, including one that suggests the state of rigor mortis could mean that Kelly wasn't killed until 10am that morning. Maxwell was adamant about the date she saw Kelly and so another mystery remains, along with many others in this case.

What is certain is, at 10.45am on Friday 9 October, the day of the Lord Mayor's Show, John McCarthy sent Thomas Bowyer, his assistant, to 13, Miller's Court to collect Kelly's outstanding rent of 29 shillings. He knocked twice at the door but there was no answer. Bowyer went around to the side to the broken window. What he saw through the window sent him racing back to McCarthy. They returned to Miller's Court and looked through the broken window together. What they beheld must have looked as though from a nightmare. Kelly had been butchered. The privacy that the cramped room had afforded the Ripper had given him free rein for his impulses.

Bowyer was immediately dispatched to Commercial Street police station. His arrival startled Inspector Walter Beck and Detective Walter Dew. Bowyer's garbled message ('Another one. Jack the Ripper. Awful') was all they needed to hear to galvanise them into action. They were at the scene by 11.00am. Unable to open the front door (Barnett said that the key had been lost sometime before, probably the night of the quarrel when the window was broken), Beck went round to the side and the broken window. Inside, an old coat was hung over the gap in the pane to keep out the draught. (Attempts to trace the coat's owner led only to Mrs Harvey, who had left some clothing with Kelly.) Beck drew it back and blanched. He stepped back and told Dew not to look. Needless to say, he did, and what he saw would haunt him for the rest of his life.

Dr Phillips arrived at 11.15am, followed by Inspector Abberline at 11.30am. The delay in opening the door can only be attributed to them. No attempt to force the door was made until 1.30pm due to the mistaken belief that the bloodhounds would soon be arriving to track the area. At 1.30pm, Dr Anderson arrived. Meanwhile, the Court had been sealed off but little else had been done. Following Anderson's command, McCarthy broke the door open with a pickaxe. The job could have been done by reaching through the broken window and releasing the catch, as Barnett and Kelly had done since the loss of the key.

McCarthy's statement that, 'It looked more like the work of a devil than of a man' seems entirely apt. The crime scene photograph that adorns almost every spine-broken book on the Ripper case, as terrible as the image it contains, cannot do justice to what they must have witnessed that day. Until

1987, it was all that we had to understand exactly what the Ripper had done to Kelly in that cramped space. Phillips' brief report at the inquest meant that there was little authentic evidence that remained and thus gave way to years of false supposition by many theorists. One of the central beliefs was that Kelly's uterus had been taken to conceal the fact that she was pregnant. Both of these claims were proved incorrect when Dr Thomas Bond's notes taken at the crime scene and the post-mortem were returned anonymously to Scotland Yard in 1987.

A brief summary and conflation of the two sets of findings should demonstrate how terrible the mutilations to Kelly's body were. Her throat was cut right down to the spinal column, the knife had notched several vertebrae. The face was mutilated by irregular slashes and the nose, cheeks, eyebrows and ears were partially removed. Both breasts had been removed by circular incisions. The intercostal muscles had been cut and the contents of the thorax were visible. The skin and tissues of the abdomen had been removed in three large flaps and the viscera removed. The right thigh had been denuded across and including outer labia and part of right buttock removed. The left thigh had been stripped to the knee and the left calf gashed. Both arms bore extensive wounds and the right thumb bore a superficial 1-inch incision. There were several abrasions on the back of the right hand and forearm. The lower part of the right lung had been torn away. The uterus, kidneys and one breast had been placed under the head. The other breast was by the right foot. The liver had been placed between the feet, the intestines by the right side of the body and the spleen by the left. The flesh from abdomen and thighs had been piled on the

bedside table. The bed and floor beneath the bed were satu-
rated with blood and the wall on the right side, in line with
the victim's neck, was marked by blood. After further investigation and the reassembly of the body by Phillips and
Bond, only one part of the body was found to be missing.
Kelly's heart.

By the time the doctors had examined the body at the
site, the news of the Ripper's latest outrage had reached the
crowds at the Lord Mayor's Show and thousands converged
on Dorset Street. Police cordons held them at bay but they
clogged the surrounding streets. Kelly's remains were
removed to Shoreditch Mortuary at around 4pm and 13,
Miller's Court was boarded up and padlocked to keep out
the curious.

The next day, Inspector Abberline returned to the Court
to examine the fireplace. The heat that it had produced
appeared to have been so fierce that it had partly melted the
solder and spout of a kettle hung above (although there is no
evidence to show that this hadn't occurred at a previous
time). All that remained in the fire were some remnants of
women's clothing. As Kelly's clothing was still piled on a
chair, it was presumed that the clothes had been those left by
Maria Harvey and that the fire had been lit by the Ripper to
help him see what he was doing.

Phillips and Bond disagreed on the time of death, both of
them estimating according to the onset of rigor mortis, the
temperature of the body and the coldness of the weather.
Bond put death at about 1–2am, Phillips much later at
5–6am. It is entirely possible that the middle period, 3–4am
is within both estimates. This suggests that the cry of
'Murder' that Mrs Prater and Mrs Lewis heard was Kelly's

final utterance. The marks on her thumb and hand certainly suggest that she attempted to fight off her attacker, if only briefly before she was overpowered. If so, it is likely that she would not have done so silently.

On the day of Kelly's discovery, Sir Charles Warren resigned. Kelly's death has often been read as the cause but, in fact, the ongoing power struggle between Warren and the Home Office over control of the Met was the main factor. Warren had written an article on 'The Police of the Metropolis' for *Murray's Magazine* and, contrary to official procedure, had not had it cleared by the Home Office before publication. Reprimanded by Matthews for this infraction, Warren tendered his resignation on 8 November. It was accepted and announced the following day and the coincidence was too good for many to read anything else into it. The radical press were especially pleased. *The Star* announced 'Whitechapel has avenged us for Bloody Sunday' and so the belief has continued. It is still felt by some theorists that Warren's squabbles with Matthews diverted his attentions from giving the Ripper case the attention it deserved.

With renewed uproar about the murders and continued cries for rewards for information leading to his capture, the Home Secretary offered a pardon to any accomplice of the Ripper who came forth with information. This can only be seen as a cynical face-saving exercise. His reasoning, that the other murders did not suggest accomplices but Kelly's did, is a blatant piece of bluster, if one considers Schwartz's testimony of Stride's murder. No one took up the offer and it continues to seem unlikely that this elusive killer ever employed an accomplice. After forcing Warren's resignation, Matthews remained, despite offers to resign. Prime Minister

Lord Salisbury believed that his resignation could only further harm his government.

The inquest into Kelly's murder was held at Shoreditch Town Hall on 12 November. The removal of Kelly's body to Shoreditch Mortuary meant that the coroner for the inquest was Dr Roderick MacDonald, Wynne Baxter's rival. Like the Eddowes inquest, it was a brief affair. Phillips' testimony was especially truncated, stating that Kelly had been found dead from 'the mortal effects of severance of the right carotid artery'. The rest of the grisly details were withheld rather than hinder the police investigation. MacDonald first hinted at an adjournment. He then stated that a verdict of the cause of death could be drawn from the evidence already given as it was not the jury's duty to uncover the murderer. The jury agreed and the verdict was given: 'Wilful murder by some person or persons unknown.'

Mary Kelly's funeral was held at St Patrick's Roman Catholic Cemetery at Leytonstone. None of her relatives were ever traced but when her coffin left the mortuary at St Leonard's, Shoreditch, a crowd of several thousand locals were there to see her off. The men removed their hats, the women wept openly and the police struggled to clear a path through the crowd so that the cortege of the hearse and two mourning coaches could proceed. Determined that she would not suffer a pauper's grave, Henry Wilton, the verger of St Leonard's, paid the entire cost of the funeral.

George Hutchinson

The early closure of the inquest unfortunately meant that one important witness never testified, and from him comes what is probably our final and clearest glimpse of Jack the Ripper. George Hutchinson, a labourer, walked into Commercial Street police station on 12 November. His information, if true, clears both Mrs Cox's man with the carroty moustache and explains who Sarah Lewis saw hanging around outside Miller's Court.

Hutchinson had been in Romford on Thursday 8 November and had walked back to London. At about 2am on 9 November he had arrived back in Whitechapel and there he met Mary Kelly at Flower and Dean Street. He had known her for about three years and 'occasionally gave her money'. Kelly asked him to lend her sixpence. He said he couldn't as he had spent all his money going down to Romford. Kelly told him that she must go and find money and they parted. Kelly headed towards Thrawl Street. A man coming in the opposite direction tapped Kelly on the shoulder and said something. They both laughed. Kelly said, 'Alright'. The man responded, 'You will be alright for what I have told you', and put his right hand around her shoulders. He had a small parcel with a strap around it in his left hand.

Hutchinson stood against the lamp by the Queen's Head pub and watched them. As they passed, the man hung his head so that his hat covered his eyes. Hutchinson stooped down to get a look at his face. 'He looked at me stern.' He followed them as they turned into Dorset Street and they stood on the corner for a few minutes. The man said something to Kelly and she replied, 'Alright, my dear. Come along, you will be comfortable.' He placed a hand on her shoulder and kissed her. She said that she had lost her handkerchief and the man pulled out a red one and gave it to her.

They then both went into Miller's Court. Hutchinson followed but could no longer see them. He waited around for about 45 minutes to see if they would re-emerge but they did not.

Impressively, Hutchinson's statement to the press the following day differs surprisingly little. He described the man as aged about 34 or 35, 5 feet 6 inches tall, of pale complexion (his press statement says 'dark') with dark eyes, dark hair and a slight moustache (press: dark and heavy) turned up at the ends. No side whiskers and his chin was clean shaven. He wore a long dark coat, its collar and cuffs trimmed with astrakhan and underneath a dark jacket, light waistcoat, white collar and black necktie with a horseshoe pin. His hat was of dark felt and turned down in the middle. He wore button boots under spats with light buttons. He had a thick gold watch chain with a big seal, a red stone hanging from it. He walked very softly and was of respectable and possibly Jewish appearance. Hutchinson was certain that he could identify him again and thought that he had seen him in Petticoat Lane on Sunday, but was not certain.

Inspector Abberline, who interrogated Hutchinson on Monday evening, was certainly impressed. Hutchinson was slow in coming forward, probably because he was spotted lurking near Miller's Court that night and this implied he was responsible for Kelly's death. The fact that he overcame his fear of being suspected of her murder and gave evidence probably convinced Abberline that he was telling the truth. He immediately sent Hutchinson out with two constables to patrol the East End. They did so until three in the morning and again on the next day but to no avail. The Ripper had vanished forever.

Jack's Back

'When the stolid English go in for a scare they take leave of all moderation and common sense. If nonsense were solid, the nonsense that was talked and written about those murders would sink a Dreadnaught.'

Robert Anderson

Following Mary Kelly's death, Joe Barnett had been interrogated for four hours, his clothing examined for bloodstains and his lodgings searched. He was released, cleared of suspicion. Throughout the winter, the police continued their investigations, although overwhelmed by the size of the task. Despite the arrest of several suspects, none was ever charged with the murders. Kelly's murder had brought a further flood of letters that had to be investigated. But with no recurrence of the Ripper's activities, a gradual winding down began to take place towards the beginning of 1889. The amateur patrols and Vigilance Committees gave up due to the long hours. The special plain-clothes patrols were disbanded around February 1889, not so much out of certainty that the Ripper was dead or locked in an asylum, but more from the financial strain of paying the extra night duty allowances. Many of the extra uniformed police drafted from other divisions were kept on, at least until the summer of the same year. There were the occasional scares that the Ripper had returned.

Rose Mylett aka Lizzie Davis

A 26-year-old prostitute, Mylett was found at 4.15am on 20 December 1888 in Clarke's Yard near Poplar High Street by PC Robert Goulding. Her body was still warm and there was no obvious sign of injury. A post-mortem revealed that there was physical evidence to suggest that she had been strangled from behind by a thin cord. The marks, however, were very faint and only covered a quarter of her neck. Despite one witness claiming Mylett had been drunk that night, no alcohol was found in her stomach. The police doubted the verdict of homicide, and were unable to find any cord near the scene. Dr Thomas Bond was asked to conduct a further post-mortem, he proposed that Mylett had choked to death while drunk, the mark on her neck caused by her stiff velvet collar. Bond's evidence was thrown out at the coroner's inquest by Wynne Baxter, who resented the intrusion. The jury brought in the same verdict as for the Ripper's victims. Robert Anderson would later write that, if not for the Jack the Ripper scare, 'no one would have thought of suggesting that it was a homicide'.

Alice McKenzie aka Clay Pipe Alice

Alice McKenzie, 40, was a charwoman and occasional prostitute. She lived at a common lodging house at 52, Gun Street with a labourer, John McCormick. On 16 July 1889, McCormick gave Alice their doss money for the night but they had quarrelled that day and Alice took the money and went out drinking. She was last seen some time between 11.30pm and midnight by a friend, Margaret Franklin.

Franklin was sitting with two other friends outside a barber's shop in Brick Lane when McKenzie hurried past. She chatted briefly but told Franklin that she could not stop.

Her body was found at 12.50am by PC Joseph Allen in Castle Alley off Whitechapel High Street. The same alley had been empty half an hour before when Allen had previously been there. McKenzie's throat had been cut, her skirts were raised and her abdomen mutilated. However, while her left carotid artery had been severed like the Ripper's other victims, the two jagged wounds did not penetrate to the spinal column, nor did they extend around the neck. The greater of the two was only 4 inches in length. The abdominal wounds were mainly no more than scratches. The deepest was seven inches and divided the skin and subcutaneous tissue without opening the abdomen itself. Whereas most evidence pointed to the Ripper being right-handed, these appeared to have been inflicted by a left-handed assailant. Bagster Phillips conducted the post-mortem with Thomas Bond making his own examination the day afterwards. Bond disagreed with Phillips' left-handed proposal and with his suggestion that the knife had been much shorter than that used on the other victims. While Phillips saw just another murder, Bond believed that the Ripper had killed McKenzie. Whether she was a victim of the Ripper or a possible copy-cat killer remains uncertain but the day of her murder saw plain-clothes detectives being redeployed on the streets of Whitechapel.

No further outrages occurred that year and in April 1890 plain-clothes police were finally withdrawn. But in February 1891 there was to be one last scare.

Frances Coles

Frances Coles was a 26-year-old prostitute who, for eight years, had managed to conceal the fact from both her elderly father and her sister, Mary Ann. They believed that she worked for a chemist. It is possible that they both had their suspicions. Mary Ann noted that on later visits her sister looked 'very poor and very dirty and sometimes smelt of drink'.

On 11 February 1891, James Thomas Sadler, a 53-year-old ship's fireman was discharged from his ship, SS Fez, and headed towards Commercial Street. Sadler had previously been a client of Coles' and they met once more in the Princess Alice. They slept together that night and spent most of the next day drinking in various pubs in the area. At some point that evening the couple quarrelled. Sadler had supposedly been mugged in Thrawl Street and had asked Coles for money. She had refused and they separated. Coles had returned to her lodgings in White's Row and passed out at the kitchen table. Sadler arrived, the worse for drink and bleeding. However, as neither he nor Coles had money to doss, the watchman encouraged first Sadler, then Coles to leave.

At around 1.45am on Friday 13 February, Coles was turned out of Shuttleworth's Eating House in Wentworth Street and headed toward Brick Lane. At 2.15am PC Ernest Thompson's first solo patrol of his career was to prove his most memorable. As he walked along Chamber Street, just off Leman Street, Thompson heard a man's footsteps walking unhurriedly away from him towards Mansell Street. He gave it no thought until, turning into Swallow Gardens, a passageway under the railway arches, he found the body of Frances Coles. Her throat had been cut and her blood still flowed. Worse, as he approached, she opened one eye. Thompson blew his whistle for assistance and, as he waited, Coles died.

Both Dr Phillips, who conducted the autopsy, and Dr Oxley, who was the first at the scene, agreed that Coles had had her throat cut after being flung to the ground. Coles' clothing had not been touched and there were no abdominal wounds. Both doctors concurred it was unlikely that the assailant had been the Ripper.

The police quickly arrested Sadler. He had returned to the White's Row lodging house at about 3.00am. He was blood-stained. He claimed he had been robbed again, this time in Ratcliffe Highway. Another witness identified Sadler as the man who had sold him a knife for a shilling and some tobacco at 10.15am that morning. After Sadler had been charged with murder on 16 February, detectives began to think carefully about the possibility that they might just have caught Jack the Ripper. It did not take long for their hopes to be dashed.

Witnesses soon cleared Sadler of being with Coles later that night and proved that his second beating, courtesy of some dock labourers, had occurred. The knife, it turned out, was so blunt when it had been sold that the witness had to sharpen it before he could use it. Witnesses also stated that Sadler had been so drunk it was unlikely that he would have been able to control his hands enough to inflict Coles' wounds. The inquest verdict of 'Murder by some person or persons unknown' cleared him. The case for Sadler being the Ripper finally fell apart when it was found that he had been at sea from 17 August to 1 October 1888.

After this point there were no more Ripper-style killings. The file at the Met remained open but suspects were thin on the ground. The Ripper disappeared into the fog of history in much the same way that movies depict him swirling off into London pea-soupers. Behind him he left the bodies of at least four women (Nichols, Chapman, Eddowes and Kelly) and quite probably six (these plus Tabram and Stride), possibly more. Ahead of him lay a century and more of theorising, arguments, backbiting, fraudulence and the mutilated corpses of several reputations.

The Suspects Assemble

> 'Theories! We were almost lost in theories; there were
> so many of them'
>
> Inspector Abberline, quoted in
> *Cassell's Saturday Journal*, 22 May 1892

'Too many Rippers and not enough corpses' could easily be
the motto of anyone hoping to solve Jack the Ripper's
crimes. The sheer wealth of possible Rippers ranges from
those considered by the police at the time right up until the
present day.

Given that various theorists could devote a whole book to
just one of these possible Rippers, we can't possibly hope to
do justice (or bring justice) to any of them. You too could be
a Ripperologist – just perm one from any of the following
then match it against the murdered prostitutes that best fit
your theory.

FBI psychological profile

In 1988 the Feds prepared a profile, specifically for the documentary 'The Secret Identity of Jack the Ripper'. It contained
the following observations: 'A local, resident male in his late
twenties. Since the murders generally occurred at weekends,
he was probably employed. Murders took place between midnight and 6am, suggesting that he was single, with no familial

ties. Of low class, since murders evinced marked unfastidious-ness. Not surgically skilled or possessing anatomical knowl-edge. Probably known to the police. Seen by acquaintances as a loner. Probably abused/deserted as a child by his mother.'

'Dr Stanley' (?–c.1918)

Fingered by Leonard Matters in *The Mystery of Jack the Ripper* (1929, reissued 1948)

The first full-length English language Ripper tome 'names' this brilliant Royal surgeon. His son supposedly caught syphilis from Mary Jane Kelly, leading to his untimely death. Once 'Stanley' had eased his grief by carving up Kelly and her associates he took a world cruise, settling in Buenos Aires in 1908. Matters' source was an unreferenced Buenos Aires journal in which an anonymous former student of Stanley's was summoned to the great man's deathbed in time to hear his confession. Daniel Farson, in *Jack the Ripper* (1972), cited a letter from a Mr Barca of Streatham. Barca claimed that a Buenos Aires dive called Sally's Bar had been reputed to be owned by Jack the Ripper. Colin Wilson would later hear from Mr AL Lee of Torquay. Mr Lee's father had supposedly met Dr Stanley while working at Golden Lane mortuary. All well and good, except Matters admitted in his book that the name was fictitious. And Kelly's post-mortem makes no mention of syphilis.

Olga Tchkersoff (?–?)

Fingered by ET Woodhall in *Jack the Ripper: Or When London Walked in Terror* (1937)

Tchkersoff was a Russian immigrant whose sister, Vera, was a prostitute who died after an abortion. Needless to say, it was all Mary Jane Kelly's fault again. The death of Olga's father from pneumonia and her mother due to alcoholism in 1888 pushed Olga over the edge and the rest is history. Possibly. After Mary Kelly's murder, Inspector Abberline postulated a 'Jill the Ripper' to his mentor, Dr Thomas Dutton. Abberline's reasoning rested mainly on Mrs Maxwell's testimony that she'd seen Kelly alive the morning after her murder. If the killer was female, she could have burned her own bloodstained clothes then worn Kelly's to leave Miller's Court, which may have accounted for Mrs Maxwell's supposed sighting, (although Kelly's clothes were reportedly found piled neatly on a chair at Miller's Court).

Another 'Jill the Ripper' theory was expounded by Sir Arthur Conan Doyle. A midwife would probably already be blood-spattered so could pass without question through the East End streets. A male killer disguised as a midwife could do so equally well. William Stewart in *Jack the Ripper – A New Theory* (1939) (and later, Ex-Detective Inspector Arthur Butler) advanced the theory that Jill was a backstreet abortionist, murdering and blackmailing prostitutes to cover up her trade. Their belief, that Kelly brought the 'mad midwife' into her house in order to abort a child she couldn't afford, falls at Dr Thomas Bond's autopsy findings that Kelly wasn't pregnant. Stewart advanced Mary Pearcey as a suspect. Like George Chapman and others (see below), she seems to have been a suspect mainly because in October 1890 she murdered her lover's wife and child. Pearcey was hanged in December 1890. Stewart saw certain similarities between Pearcey's m.o. (slit throats, killing in private and dumping bodies in a public place) and the Whitechapel murderer. Tom Cullen suggested Stewart had overlooked the possibility of a vengeful lesbian lover. He singled out Kelly's friend, Maria Harvey as the possible culprit, although she reportedly left before Barnett was ejected.

There was also 'the nurse'. Appalled at finding out that her husband had gone with a prostitute, she set out to avenge herself upon the women who threatened her marriage. And speaking of medical types and Russians…

Dr Alexander Pedachenko (1857?-1908?)

Fingered by William Le Queux in *Things I Know About Kings, Celebrities and Crooks* (1923) and expanded upon by Donald McCormick in *The Identity of Jack the Ripper* (1959)

Bear with us, this is a good one. Pedachenko lived in Walworth with his sister. Along with a friend Levitski (who wrote the Ripper letters) and a seamstress Miss Winberg (who engaged the victims in conversation), Pedachenko killed prostitutes under orders from Ochrana (the then Russian secret police). Their aim was to discredit the Met, whom they hated for tolerating emigrant dissidents and anarchists in the East End. When their plan succeeded (with the resignation of Sir Charles Warren), Pedachenko was smuggled back to Moscow and exiled to Yakutsk (or sent to an asylum after trying to murder a woman in Russia). Le Queux claimed the information came from a manuscript entitled *Great Russian Criminals*, written by Rasputin. Pedachenko, supposedly, was an alias for Vassily Konovalov and, as well as being a surgeon, he was an occasional transvestite. He was wearing women's clothing when he was arrested in Russia. An unsourced letter, attributed to Sir Basil Thomson (assistant commissioner of the Met 1913–1919), states that Konovalov also used the alias 'Mikhail Ostrog'. It seems unlikely that Konovalov was the Michael Ostrog the Met sought at the time of the Ripper murders.

Donald McCormick furthered the madness by quoting from Dr Thomas Dutton's unpublished notebooks (themselves not seen since 1935) that Pedachenko was the double of Severin Klosowski (see below). Both barber's assistants, they knew each other and would exchange identities for their nightly excursions. Hope that's clear, then.

Another Russian candidate was Nicolay Vasiliev (also called Nicolas Vassili, Vassily, Vasilyeff and Nicolai Wassili). He was mentioned in the British and international press, as well as in two American books on the Whitechapel murders, published between October and December 1888. Having become a leader of the Skoptsy (a Russian religious cult that preached castration), Vasiliev fled to Paris in 1872, at the age of 25, to evade persecution by the Russian government. He spent his time trying to convert prostitutes, including one known as 'Madeleine' with whom he fell in love. When she left him he tracked her down and killed her before butchering another seven prostitutes. Caught when his next victim called for help, Vasiliev was tried and sent to an asylum (in either Russia or France) for the next sixteen years. He was released on 1 January 1888 and announced his intention to move to London. Here he lived with friends in Whitechapel until Polly Nichols was killed. Since then, papers reported that 'his friends have not seen him'. The problem with Vasiliev is that no-one may have ever seen him. An article in the *London Star* for 17 November 1888, entitled 'A Fictional French "Ripper"' relayed doubts about his story. It quoted an interview with M Macé, a former head of the Sureté, who stated that no such murders occurred in Paris in 1872. This seemingly conclusive rubbishing did little to stop other papers continuing to print and embellish Vasiliev's tale. In an essay on the articles for www.casebook.co.uk, Stepan Poberowski notes that several of these articles resemble stories planted in other newspapers by the Ochrana. These articles, he suggests, were part of a provocation campaign to force the Met to interrogate Russian immigrants. Any information gathered would be fed back to the Ochrana via their spies at Scotland Yard. If Vasiliev was a fictional tool of provocation, his usefulness ended when the murders stopped. By January 1889 newspapers no longer mentioned him, and there is no indication that he was ever actively sought as a genuine suspect.

Montague John Druitt (1857–1888)

Fingered by Tom Cullen in *Autumn of Terror* (1965), Daniel Farson in *Jack the Ripper* (1972), Martin Howells and Keith Skinner in *The Ripper Legacy* (1987), John Wilding in *Jack the Ripper Revealed* (1993)

One of three suspects proposed by Sir Melville Macnaghten, who became assistant Chief Constable of the CID six months after Mary Kelly's murder. The document, known as 'the Macnaghten Memoranda' was discovered by Daniel Farson in 1959 and was written ostensibly to discredit *The Sun*'s Thomas Cutbush theory (see also: Kosminski, Ostrog).

A barrister, schoolmaster, gentleman and cricket ace, Druitt's body was fished from the Thames at Chiswick on 31 December 1888. It had been in the water for approximately a month and there were four large stones in the coat pockets. A note to his brother, William, read to the effect: 'Since Friday I felt that I was going to be like mother [i.e. incarcerated in an asylum] and it would be best for all concerned if I were to die.'

Melancholia was a common trait in the family. Several of Druitt's immediate family had attempted or committed suicide. On or around 30 November, Druitt, for reasons unknown, was fired from his teaching post. William later learned that Druitt had been dismissed after getting into serious trouble at the school. The cause of this trouble is unclear but it seems to have been the final straw. By the time William was told of his absence from chambers, Druitt had already been missing, probably dead, for over a week.

There is no real evidence to suggest that Druitt was the Ripper. Sir Melville Macnaghten appears to be the first to really push for him as a suspect. But the only proof behind his conviction of Druitt's guilt is unspecified 'private information (from which) I have little doubt but that his own family believed him to have been the murderer'. What information, and from what source, was lost when Macnaghten later destroyed all his personal papers relating to the matter. Further difficulties arise. Druitt was a tall, slim Anglo-Saxon, which goes against the bulk of eyewitness descriptions. Nor is there a clear way to place Druitt in the East End. Several of his cricket engagements (one in Dorset) clash with the times of the murders.

In 1961, Daniel Farson went to Australia in search of a

document that supposedly proved Druitt's guilt. 'The East End Murderer – I Knew Him' was allegedly written by his cousin Lionel, a doctor who had emigrated in 1886. Such tantalising evidence, as is often the case, proved to be a hoax. There remains nothing solid to place Druitt as Jack. Abberline was certainly unimpressed by the theory. When asked about Druitt in 1903, he said, 'You can state most emphatically that Scotland Yard is really no wiser on the subject than it was fifteen years ago. It is simple nonsense to talk of the police having proof that the man is dead.'

What ties Druitt to the Ripper is his timely suicide. Unexplained matters such as the increasingly violent mutilations and the sudden cessation of the murders are neatly cleared up in Macnaghten's theory that 'the murderer's brain gave way altogether after his awful glut in Miller's Court' as a result of which he either committed suicide or was committed by relatives (see Kosminski). A major issue with this solution is that serial killers rarely tend to commit suicide, but keep killing until, by luck or design, they are caught. Another suicide, Edward Buchan, was chosen by Roger Barber for 'Did Jack the Ripper Commit Suicide?' (*Criminologist*, Autumn 1990). Buchan ran a marine store (or was a cobbler) in Poplar and obligingly killed himself on 19 November 1888.

Aaron Kosminski (1864/65–1919)

Along with his championing of Druitt, Macnaghten was also the first to suggest Kosminski as a suspect. A Polish Jewish hairdresser, he was certified insane and committed to Colney Hatch Lunatic Asylum in 1891. He'd been suffering from periods of insanity for three years and roamed the streets, eating food out of the gutter. He heard voices and had once threatened his sister with a knife. However, usually Kosminski's insanity sent him into a torpor, during which time he refused to bathe or to work. Plus, he remained insane and at liberty until 1891 while the murders ceased in 1888. Far from being Macnaghten's 'homicidal lunatic with a deep hatred of women', Kosminski's medical records assert that he was neither suicidal nor dangerous to others. Apart from the knife incident, Kosminski's only other act of violence was in 1892, when he threw a chair at an asylum attendant. This did nothing to alter the authorities' opinions that he was harmless. In addition, his build, small and slight, doesn't fit the majority of most Ripper descriptions.

In July 2006, Chief Inspector Donald Swanson's great-grandson donated the book containing the 'Swanson marginalia' to Scotland Yard's 'Black Museum'. Originally discovered by his grandson when the book passed to him around 1980, the notes were first published in the *Daily Telegraph* in 1987. Swanson's handwritten note is in the margin and end-page of his copy of Commissioner Robert Anderson's controversial memoirs, published in 1910. In these, Anderson sketchily described the suspect whom he believed to be the Ripper. Anderson's description of the man extends little beyond mentioning he was a low-class Polish Jew from Whitechapel whose relatives shielded him from the police. He also states that 'the only person who ever saw the murderer unhesitatingly identified the suspect the instant he was confronted with him; but he refused to give evidence against him'. Swanson's notes continue, mentioning that the witness, also a Jew, refused to give evidence against the suspect as he did not want to be 'the means of the murderer being hanged'. Swanson also states that the '…suspect had been identified at the Seaside Home where he had been sent to us with difficulty in order to subject him to identification and he knew he was identified.' The 'Seaside Home' was one of the Convalescent Police Seaside Homes. The first of these was opened in West Brighton in March 1890. If this is the correct location a period of eighteen months had passed since the original sighting of Kosminski, sixteen months alone would have passed since the last murder. The 'marginalia' further details that Kosminski was taken 'to Colney Hatch and died shortly afterwards' when, in fact, he lived on until 1919. Despite these anomalies, Swanson's notations are clearly for personal consumption only. Thus, having no agenda to mislead anyone, they simply relate the truth as Swanson saw it from 1910. The marginalia's provenance is unquestionably from Swanson's own hand. Despite Macnaghten's, Anderson's and Swanson's enthusiasm for Kosminski-as-the-Ripper, there exists as much evidence against him as any of our other suspects.

There were other mentally-ill suspects. Aaron Davis Cohen (aka David Cohen and possibly aka Nathan Kaminsky) was an extremely violent lunatic whose capture and incarceration came closely after the cessation of the murders and who might possibly have been confused by Macnaghten with Kosminski. There was the religious maniac, G Wentworth Bell Smith who terrified his landlord with his nightly excursions and his fulminations on drowning prostitutes. Contemporary Ripper theorist Dr L Forbes Winslow was convinced of his guilt and continually raised this with police. There was also borderline psychotic butcher, Jacob Levy, who may have been recognised talking to Catharine Eddowes by fellow butcher Joseph Levy near the Church Passage entrance to Mitre Square. And perhaps that explains Joseph's apparent reluctance to come forward at the inquest.

Thomas Cutbush (suspected by *The Sun* in 1894) was arrested after escaping from an asylum and stabbing two women in the bottom. Neither his knife, nor his method match the Ripper's, but he had contracted syphilis from a prostitute early in 1888 and suffered from religious mania and nightly wanderings. Although police were reasonably convinced. Macnaghten wrote his memorandum partly to rubbish the Cutbush theory. But then, he would, suggests AP Wolf (in *Jack The Myth* [1993]) because he was covering up for Cutbush's uncle, a senior police officer. The uncle would later shoot himself...

Michael Ostrog (1833?-?)

While the police were certainly actively seeking Michael Ostrog during the murders, it seems more likely that they sought to eliminate him from enquiries rather than seriously considered him the Ripper. Ostrog was a Russian conman who adopted a host of identities, all with hard-luck stories of exile and poverty attached. With these he continually duped society figures into providing him with cash and lodgings. He often stole their possessions. His crimes in Britain began in Oxford in 1863 and he continued, with breaks at Her Majesty's Pleasure, until at least 1888 (movements have been traced to 1904 by researcher Derryl Goffee). Ostrog's confidence tricks appear to be the trigger for police interest. At a time when much expert opinion suggested the killer was a lunatic who possessed anatomical knowledge, Ostrog's lies put him in both categories. He frequently told his marks that he was a former surgeon, and often feigned insanity to avoid being sent to prison. Beyond one incident when he threatened an arresting officer with a loaded revolver, a propensity to violence appears non-existent. His height of 5 feet 11 inches, notably tall for the period, seems to put him out of the range of the Ripper sightings. His ability to charm several society women would suggest that he was a ladykiller of another kind entirely.

Other suspected 'foreign-looking' (or sounding) men include a lethal tag-team triumvirate of Portuguese sailors proposed by contemporary theorist and police-irritant, EK Larkins. You didn't have to be Portuguese, however. Sausage maker and self-described surgeon Alios Szmeredy committed suicide in Vienna while under arrest for murder. Rumours in Austria that he had been the Ripper resulted in Carl Muusmann's *Hvem Var Jack the Ripper?* (1908), arguably the first book-length attempt to identify Jack. Itinerant Swede Nikolaus Benelius was arrested after unlawfully entering an East End house and grinning at the female occupant. 'Fogelma' was described as being a Norwegian sailor prone to madness in *Empire News* (23 October 1923). Committed to the Morris Plains Lunatic Asylum, New Jersey in 1899 (although no records of his incarceration exist), he would mutter about events that 'connected him clearly with the atrocious crimes of 1888'. A pity he doesn't seem to have actually existed.

The Argentinean businessman, Alonzo Maduro, had his identity divulged in 1952 by a Mr Salway who had met him in Whitechapel just before Emma Smith's death. Maduro had told him that all prostitutes should be killed. After Mary Kelly's death, Salway claimed he had found knives in Maduro's possession.

Severin Klosowski/George Chapman (1865–1903)

Fingered in R Michael Gordon's *Alias Jack the Ripper* (2001). Abberline's suspect. Considered strongly by Philip Sugden in *The Complete History of Jack the Ripper* (1994)

One thing is certain about Klosowski – he did murder women. Between 1895 and 1901 he poisoned three successive wives with antimony (which, he believed, left no trace). For these crimes, he was tried and hanged in 1903. The more the trial revealed about Klosowski's background, the more convinced Inspector Abberline was that he was Jack the Ripper. Klosowski was a qualified junior surgeon who had been a barber's assistant in Whitechapel during the murders, emigrating to America in mid-1890. During his stay in New Jersey, a prostitute was strangled and mutilated in Manhattan. This immediately sparked rumours that the Ripper had emigrated, but there is no proof that Klosowski was even in Manhattan. He returned to London in 1891–2 where he resumed his career as a barber.

The similarities between his appearance and eyewitness descriptions are notable, particularly that of George Hutchinson. Klosowski also fits many criteria supplied in the FBI's profile. He was charming and violent towards women, and sadistic enough to slowly poison his three victims. His callousness towards his wives' suffering was noted by more than one witness. He threatened his first wife, Lucy Baderski, with a knife more than once. At the best estimate, he had first emigrated to the East End around eighteen months before the beginning of the crimes; long enough to acquaint himself with the area and pick up some conversational English. Moreover, he favoured a sailor's cap and carried a little bag...

It's said, when Klosowski was convicted, Abberline turned to Inspector Godley, the arresting officer, and said: 'You've got Jack the Ripper at last!' However, Klosowski was only 23 when the crimes were committed, much younger than any witness description estimated. More problematic is the switch from one *modus operandi* to another. Serial killers have been known to experiment with other methods. The Yorkshire Ripper, Peter Sutcliffe, briefly switched from killing his victims with a hammer to strangling them with a piece of flex to divert police attention from the fact that he was still killing but soon reverted. To accept that Klosowski was Jack the Ripper we have to believe that he was capable of switching from viciously mutilating prostitutes to poisoning his wives. A change in behaviour that great is a serious leap.

Another poisoner got in on the act: Dr Thomas Neil Cream was hanged for the poisoning of four prostitutes in Lambeth in 1892. As the trapdoor opened, he is alleged to have said, 'I am Jack the...' (Relax, he was actually in jail in America at the time of the killings.) Other wife murderers include William Henry Bury. He stabbed his wife to death in Glasgow in 1889 but had lived at Bow during the previous year. Graffiti outside his lodgings claimed that 'Jack the Ripper is at the back of this door'. Frederick Bailey Deeming killed two wives, one in Liverpool (as well as his children) in 1891, a second in Australia in 1892. He was said

to have confessed to the last two Ripper crimes. His solicitor denied it.

James Kelly killed his wife in 1883. Doctors doubted he
was insane but he was locked up in Broadmoor anyway. He
escaped in January 1888 but turned himself in in 1927,
remaining in Broadmoor until his death. James Tully's theory
(*The Secret of Prisoner 1167* [1997]) is that Kelly killed his
wife when she discovered his affair with Mary Kelly. He
escaped Broadmoor to find that Mary had aborted the child
she was bearing him. He killed each woman after asking
about her whereabouts and finally Mary herself. Supposedly,
the authorities were so embarrassed by his escape they covered the whole thing up.

Prince Albert Victor Christian Edward ('Prince Eddy') (1864–92)

Fingered by Phillippe Julien in *Edouard VII* (1962) and Dr
Thomas Stowell in 'Jack the Ripper – A Solution?'
(*Criminologist*, November 1970). Stowell coyly identified the
Ripper as 'Mr S' and later denied, despite obvious inferences
in the article, that he had ever suggested Eddy was the
Ripper. Cleared by Michael Harrison in *Clarence: The Life of
HRH The Duke of Clarence and Avondale 1864–1892* (1972)

Grandson of Queen Victoria, Duke of Clarence and
Avondale from 1891, Prince Eddy was rumoured to be the
Ripper after syphilis destroyed his mental faculties. His
experience as a deer hunter gave him the skill to eviscerate
his victims (and may first have provided him with a sexual
awakening). A cover-up concealed the facts from the public
and thus saved the Royal family.

What was not covered up were various Court Circulars and journals that placed him conclusively in Yorkshire, Scotland and Sandringham during the murders. Eddy died of pneumonia in 1892, unless Melvyn Fairclough was correct in his assertion in *The Ripper and The Royals* (1991) that he was held a deranged prisoner at Glamis Castle until the 1930s.

Of course, you don't have to be a public figure to be suspected of being Jack the Ripper, but it does seem to help. Those accused at different times include: George Gissing, author of *New Grub Street*; William Gladstone, whose attempts to help fallen women were renowned; Frank Miles, 1880s Turner Prize winner, known for paedophile leanings, who suffered from dementia from 1887; Dr Thomas Barnardo, who did meet Liz Stride and was rumoured to have kept a diary (hmm) in which the dates of murders were left blank; Lord Randolph Churchill (another of Joseph Gorman Sickert's Rippers – see below); Madame Blavatsky, founder of Theosophy; opium-addicted visionary poet Francis Thompson who may have committed the murders in a frenzy of religious symbolism; and let's not forget the sadistic harlot mutilator that was... Lewis Carroll.

Sir William Withey Gull (1816–90)

Fingered by Joseph Sickert in the BBC dramatised investigation of the case *Jack the Ripper* (1973) and by Stephen Knight in *Jack the Ripper: The Final Solution* (1977)

Gull was an eminent physician, an ardent vivisectionist and (according to Stephen Knight) a prominent Freemason (although the Masons have always denied it). In 1873 he identified and named anorexia nervosa. He became physician-in-ordinary to Queen Victoria in 1887.

Thomas Stowell places Gull pursuing Eddy through Whitechapel in order to certify him insane, but this, according to Gorman Sickert, was not the true story. A brief summary of the story he told to Knight, and Knight tells us: Prince Eddy secretly married a shop girl, Annie Elizabeth Crook (Sickert's real grandmother), and she bore him a daughter, Alice Margaret Crook. When the relationship was discovered, Annie Crook was abducted by Crown agents and committed to an asylum. (In reality, she spent much of her later life in workhouses.) The daughter was saved by the artist, Walter Sickert, Joseph Sickert's alleged grandfather and a close friend of Prince Eddy. Mary Kelly, an acquaintance of Sickert's, found out. Along with Liz Stride, Annie Chapman and Polly Nichols, she attempted to blackmail the Crown. Queen Victoria and the Prime Minister, Lord Salisbury, fearing that the revelations would lead to revolution, sent Gull to rid them of the meddlesome whores. Gull enlisted the help of a coachman, John Netley, to aid his scheme. When it was finished, Gull was secretly committed by Salisbury and other members of his lodge. At the same time, his death was announced. Through complex machinations, Druitt was selected as a fall guy.

The story told by Joseph Gorman Sickert to Stephen Knight is a rattling tale – royalty, sex, violence, and just when you think it can't get any more preposterous, it does, bless it. Sickert stated that he was the offspring of Walter Sickert and Alice Margaret Crook, who began an affair after her husband, a man named Gorman, had proven impotent. Knight brought a wealth of Masonic theory and valuable

Ripper research to the tale. This included a long-lost statement by Israel Schwartz. Schwartz's testimony led to Knight's conclusion that Walter Sickert had worked as Gull's look-out man. Possibly because of this revelation, Gorman Sickert later publicly withdrew most of his story. Despite a rapturous reception from many quarters, Knight's theory later fell out of favour. Although the fact that it was ever accepted as anything other than a rattling good pot-boiler suggests that Ripperology is not always the most rigorous of sciences.

Knight died of an inoperable brain tumour in 1985, by which time he'd joined the Rajneesh cult and written a further exposé of Freemasonry, *The Brotherhood* (1983). Sickert continued to change and embroider his story for whoever was listening but it appears to have followed the law of diminishing returns. In 1981, after the arrest of the Yorkshire Ripper, Sickert claimed that Sutcliffe had once tried to run him down with his lorry.

Walter Richard Sickert (1860–1942)

Fingered by Jean Overton Fuller in *Sickert and The Ripper Crimes* (1990) and Patricia Cornwell in *Portrait of a Killer: Jack the Ripper — Case Closed* (2002)

Sickert was a renowned British artist, born in Munich. His work, and that of his followers, found a space between French impressionism and realism, drawing inspiration from London's seedy music halls and down-at-heel lodging houses. Although not considered independently in the previous edition, Sickert had already been unmasked by Fuller in 1990. Rightly or wrongly, what got him noticed as a suspect was Cornwell's book. This situation seems to have occurred simply by virtue of being in the area and being famous.

As noted under Sir William Gull's entry above, Jean Overton Fuller writes in *Sickert and the Ripper Crimes* that the 'royal baby story' (Gull and all) was related to her mother, the artist Violet Overton Fuller, in 1948. She claimed to have heard it from Florence Pash, a fellow artist and close friend of Sickert. Supposedly, Ms Pash's suspicions were aroused by Sickert's claim to have seen the bodies and his detailed descriptions of the wounds. Yet this knowledge could be gained by following the case closely through the newspapers and Sickert was a voracious reader. That the Whitechapel Murders fascinated Sickert is without question. He frequently lunched out with the story of how he had rented a room previously occupied by a 'pale veterinary student' who was collected by his parents in the middle of the night shortly after Mary Kelly's death. The landlady told Sickert that it was only after he left that she realised he was... Go on, guess. This tale became *The Lodger* after Marie Belloc Lowndes heard it from Sickert. Tales of murder fuelled Sickert's creativity but reading about the Ripper isn't the same as being the Ripper.

Pash's tale fits very neatly with Stephen Knight's theory in *The Final Solution*. Perhaps a little too neatly, as Pash, Fuller claims, also relates the story of Lord Salisbury allegedly paying Sickert £500 for an inferior painting – clearly a bribe to buy Sickert's secrecy. Knight and Pash both claimed that the prime minister was part of the Freemasons' plot. Yet Lord Salisbury was never a freemason. Also, Sickert told the same story, but about another artist, A Vallon. Lord

Salisbury had paid the painter off personally because he disliked the family portrait he had commissioned. This confusion suggests that Pash's evidence may not be all it seems.

On the subject of paintings, Fuller's (and Pash's) story includes the same detail about Sickert including a clue in one of his works. In at least one of the versions of 'Ennui' (Sickert painted five, possibly more) a painting on the wall behind the ennui-laden couple depicts a statue of Queen Victoria. Perched on its shoulder is a seagull… However, Jean Fuller insists that it is a bluff, a deliberately false lead placed there by Sickert to lead suspicion away from himself and put Gull in the frame. As Alan Moore points out in *From Hell*, given that Fuller's favoured suspect was Sickert, why include Pash's detail about the clue in the first place? Would it not have been simpler to find another 'clue' that points to Sickert?

Patricia Cornwell does just that, and using another version of 'Ennui'. In this version, the painting on the wall depicts a young woman. Cornwell notes that behind her there appears to be a man lurking in the shadows, or what may be an ear, anyway. This is read as Sickert admitting to his guilt. As clues go, it is hardly the gold standard. If it can be said to be a clue at all.

Far from being part of a royalist plot to cover up an illegitimate child, Sickert, insists Cornwell, was a remorseless scopophiliac psychopath who committed the murders alone. He was an amateur thespian, a continual self-reinventor, a lover of disguise (all which helped him slip through the crowds unrecognized). He was a tireless self-promoter and continually wrote freelance articles and letters to the editors of many UK papers. He was also an appalling snob, profligate with money and an inveterate skirt-chaser. His restless intellect and prolific creativity meant that he was easily able to elude the police investigation and continually taunt them with letters in which he effortlessly disguised his handwriting while all the while dropping clues as to his identity and whereabouts. Clues that the police were too occupied to pick up on. Cornwell reckons that out of the many Ripper letters received by the authorities, the majority were penned by Sickert.

Cornwell states that as a child Sickert had suffered several operations on his penis to correct a fistula which had left his penis brutally truncated and sexually useless. Thus disfigured, Sickert as an adult was probably mocked by a prostitute at some point and this proved to be the catalyst for the later murders. Unfortunately, there are no surviving medical records to prove that these operations ever actually took place, or that Sickert's genitalia were ever disfigured. On the contrary, rumours abound that Sickert was very much a ladies' man and fathered several illegitimate children.

Portrait of a Killer proposes that Sickert began killing with Martha Tabram (called Tabran throughout) and didn't stop after Mary Kelly. Instead he varied his methods, killing all of the Ripper's proposed later victims (see Chapter 7) as well as being responsible for, among others, the murder of an eight-year-old girl in Newcastle (6 August 1889), 'The Whitehall Mystery' (3 October 1888) and human remains dumped in Middlesbrough docks (13 December 1889). He also killed prostitute Emily Dimmock in Camden in 1907 and depicted the subject afterwards in such paintings as 'Persuasion' and 'Jack the Ripper's Bedroom'. Cornwell makes no secret that it was her dislike of Sickert's paintings that led her to suspect him in the first place.

It is impossible to read *Portrait of a Killer* without becoming immediately aware of Cornwell's personality. Her authorial voice continually intrudes on the (admittedly well-beaten) narrative as if she is trying to paper over the cracks in her theory. Sometimes this is to good effect and her side-bars on the actual methods of modern forensics would arguably have made a much better book. Her attempts to humanize the victims can only be applauded in an industry where they have become little more than bloody chess pieces. However, more often Cornwell adopts a hectoring tone that suggests you're being harangued by a slightly-obsessed fan of *CSI*.

While there is no doubt that Cornwell has unearthed some interesting links between Sickert and the Ripper, that final, conclusive link that merges the two personalities is a very long way off. Sickert, with his obsession with murder in general and the Ripper in particular, has partially succeeded in weaving himself into Ripper mythology. When painting he would wear a red scarf, telling friends that it had belonged to one of Jack's victims. Cornwell's assertion that Sickert 'identified' with the Ripper may be cause for concern, but he was not alone in this. False confessors such as John Fitzgerald and Alfred Blanchard readily supplied details of 'their' crimes to any enquirers. The day Blanchard confessed, he spent all day in a pub, answering questions on the subject from his fellow drinkers. But identifying is not the same as actually being. Sickert had done some acting earlier in his life and there is no doubt that he never lost his sense of 'The Great Dramatic Moment'. What could be more dramatic than being inside the mind of the Ripper (except, perhaps, shocking one's friends a little)?

Sickert's body was cremated, leaving no DNA against which to check possible saliva on Ripper envelopes and stamps. On a positive note, the rumours that Cornwell cut up several of Sickert's paintings searching for DNA samples are not borne out in the book. Some of Sickert's own letters are tested but, as Cornwell ruefully points out, the gum could well have been wet with a sponge. A result on mitochondrial DNA reveals a connection between one of Sickert's letters and one of the Ripper letters 'specific enough to eliminate 99% of the population'. Sadly, she doesn't mention the population of where, exactly. Perhaps this will be addressed in the proposed sequel.

For a more detailed dissection of Cornwell's theory, we suggest that you try 'Patricia Cornwell and Walter Sickert: A Primer' by Stephen P Ryder on the inestimable Casebook website (see address below). Matthew Sturgis's 2005 biography of Sickert (*Walter Sickert: A Life*) provides a more sober account of the artist's life.

Joseph Barnett (1858–1926)

Fingered by Bruce Paley in *Jack the Ripper – The Simple Truth* (1996)

Mary Jane Kelly's lover, Barnett, was the fourth of five children. His father, a fish porter, died when he was six. His mother appears to have deserted the family soon afterwards. Barnett was brought up by his elder brothers, Daniel and Denis, and his sister Catherine. It is believed that becoming an orphan caused Barnett's speech defect, echolalia, which caused him to compulsively repeat the last few words of anything said to him.

Paley advances his theory cautiously but persuasively. He points out that, unlike most suspects, Barnett fits the description in the FBI profile. Barnett's rationale for the killings is to stop Kelly continuing as a prostitute. His dislike of Kelly's trade is certainly made clear in both his and others' statements at Kelly's inquest. Paley suggests that, after Kelly's murder and the four-hour-long interrogation that Barnett underwent, he no longer had the motive or the nerve, to commit further murders.

Two other men in Mary Kelly's life have been put forward as possible Rippers: John McCarthy, her landlord, and Joseph Fleming, her old lover. Fleming is suspected because of the possibility that a Joseph Fleming who died in 1920 at Claybury Mental Hospital was the same man.

James Kenneth Stephen (1859–92)

Fingered in Michael Harrison's *Clarence* (1972), David Abrahamsen's *Murder and Madness: The Secret Life of Jack the Ripper* (1992) and John Wilding's *Jack the Ripper Revealed* (1993)

Prince Eddy's tutor while at Cambridge, 1883, Stephen suffered a blow to the head in 1886 which would later cause brain damage and his subsequent death in 1892. A noted orator, Stephen never settled on one career, moving from don to journalist to lawyer. He returned to residence at Cambridge in 1890. There is no real evidence linking Stephen to the Ripper murders. Arguably, Harrison's book names him merely because he was exonerating Prince Eddy and wanted to give his readers an alternative. He speculated that Eddy and Stephen became lovers while Eddy was at

Cambridge. Once the relationship necessarily ceased, Stephen embarked on his murderous career, committing the crimes on dates that would taunt Eddy. Harrison notes signs of misogyny and sadism in Stephen's poetry. Abrahamsen proposes that both Stephen and Eddy were the Ripper, clearly disagreeing with Harrison's various alibis for Eddy. Wilding teams Stephen up with Druitt to no more convincing effect.

James Maybrick (1838–1889)

Fingered by his own 'diary' and Shirley Harrison in *The Diary of Jack the Ripper* (1993/1998)

A drug-addicted Liverpudlian cotton merchant, Maybrick hit the headlines after his death in 1889 when his wife Florence was arrested and tried for his murder. Maybrick had often used arsenic and toxins as stimulants and aphrodisiacs yet these facts were little considered during his wife's trial. In one of many connections that the Ripper case seems to revel in, Florence Maybrick's trial was presided over by Sir James Stephen, the father of JK Stephen. At that point Sir James was on the verge of insanity and did not grasp the importance of much of the trial evidence. Florence's own admission of adultery certainly prejudiced the case against her and she was found guilty. Fifteen years later she was reprieved.

Maybrick's association with the Ripper only began in 1991 when Michael Barrett was handed a journal by his friend Tony Devereaux. Beyond assuring him it was genuine, Devereaux told Barrett nothing. The journal consists of 63 handwritten pages in an old scrapbook. It was Barrett who identified the author as Maybrick and took it to Doreen Montgomery at literary agents Rupert Crew. Since then barrages of tests have been taken on the ink, the handwriting and the details. Some have 'proved' its age, some have not. In June 1994, Barrett confessed to forging the diary, a statement withdrawn by his solicitors. They claimed that he was not in his right mind at the time of the admission. Comparisons with Maybrick's handwriting suggest he didn't write the diary. One cautiously advanced theory is that the writer knew him well, because of the inclusion of many personal details of his life. But whether the purpose was to incriminate Maybrick, or merely to forge a legend, is unknown. The diary entries certainly contain factual errors concerning the murders, including the canard about objects arranged at Annie Chapman's feet. They also contain a risible amount of handwritten laughter. The discovery of a watch in 1993, which had scratched in its inner case Maybrick's name, the phrase 'I am Jack' and the initials of the canonical victims has only created further factions in Ripperology. The carvings have apparently tested as historically correct. The books supporting Maybrick as the Ripper adopt a worrying hectoring tone which emphasise the rifts in this grisly 'science'. A documentary, *The Diary of Jack the Ripper*, was made in 1993. Hosted by Michael Winner and featuring various 'experts', it draws no final conclusion about Maybrick's other career.

Dr Frances Tumblety

Fingered by Stewart Evans and Paul Gainey in *The Lodger* (1995)

Born in Ireland, Tumblety's family, including eleven children, emigrated to Rochester, New York State, during his
childhood. He learned about medicine from a local doctor
described as 'disreputable'. In 1850, Tumblety set himself up
as a herb doctor in Detroit. He remained financially secure
until his death. Rumours of charlatanism were never far
behind nor were those of his preference for young men and
his ill-concealed misogyny. Tumblety was run out of Boston
when a patient of his died and the coroner's inquest marked
this down to gross malpractice. He was arrested in London,
on 7 November 1888 and charged with eight counts of gross
indecency and indecent assault with force and arms against
four men. Bailed on 16 November, he fled the country four
days later. Calling himself Frank Townsend, he arrived in
America just in time to find the newspapers heaving with
suspicions that he was the Ripper. When Inspector Walter
Andrews (who, along with Abberline, was seconded to the
Whitechapel investigation) arrived in America, Tumblety
fled again. He surfaced in 1893, living with his sister and
died in St Louis in 1903. His height (5 feet 10 inches) and
prodigious moustache would seem to rule him out of the
Ripper race.

Another slight problem is the matter of his arrest on 7
November, which effectively puts him out of the way for
Mary Kelly's murder. Evans and Gainey suggest a solution.
A rumour in the American press of the time was that
Tumblety had first been arrested on charges of being the
Ripper. If this was the case then the police would have
released him in time to kill Mary Kelly. Only ten days later
did they place him under a 'holding charge' of indecent
assault. After Tumblety's death, a collection of preserved

uteruses was found amongst his possessions.

Many other medical men have fallen under suspicion. Dr John Hewitt, who was confined to Coton Hill Asylum during 1888, was considered, in 1995, to be Sickert's unnamed veterinary student (see above). Although Hewitt was released from the asylum several times during 1888, it was proven that no occasions match the dates of the murders. Dr William Thomas of Anglesey was the Ripper according to continued local oral tradition. He practised about three-quarters of a mile from Buck's Row, and supposedly returned home to Aberffraw unexpectedly after each murder. He suffered a breakdown and poisoned himself in 1889. Dr William Westcott was outed as a suspect in 1992 mainly because he was a founder of the Order of the Golden Dawn and the authors detected ritualism in the murders. Dr Rosalyn D'Onston (real name Robert Onston Stephenson) started out as a Ripper-hunter, tracking his suspect, one Dr Morgan Davies, but then turned hunted when he was reported to the police by his assistant and, much later, fingered by Melvin Harris in *The True Face of Jack the Ripper* (1994) and later still by Ivor Edwards in *Jack the Ripper's Black Magic Rituals* (2003). The most recent doctor to come under scrutiny is:

Dr John Williams (1840–1926)

Fingered by Tony Williams with Humphrey Price in *Uncle Jack* (2005)

Or 'The John Williams?' as someone asks the author at one point in his narrative. By this they mean another one of several doctors to the royal family and the driving force behind the National Library of Wales. Just in case you thought they were talking about the composer of the music for *Jaws*, which would be outlandish even by Ripper-theory standards.

This John Williams was an obstetrician. His outspokenness and his arrogance did little to endear him to colleagues or to slow his career's progress at University College Hospital. His unlikable character led to rumours of nepotism, although these may have been engendered partly by jealousy over his financial success. He rose through the medical ranks to be eventually appointed surgeon accoucher to Princess Beatrice. He was the doctor who delivered 'The Lost Prince'. The mention that he became a Freemason is a blind as far as Ripper theories go.

The author, having uncovered the truth in a dismayingly large font size, seems a little uncomfortable at pointing the finger at such a distinguished ancestor (Uncle Jack was in fact his grandmother's great-great-uncle, but that many 'greats' on a book-jacket may invite disrespectful comparison with the material inside). This perhaps explains his focus on the medical research aspect of the doctor's crimes. While not exactly downplaying the murders themselves, the book is one of a handful that does not carry the depressingly-familiar mortuary photographs of the victims.

At the National Library of Wales, Williams the author stumbled across a cache of his ancestor's papers. A notebook provides Williams the doctor's records of his patients. Among them is an entry about performing an abortion on 'Mary Anne Nichols' in 1885. Passing over that 'e', the author begins to wonder... According to his theory, Williams the doctor was trapped in a loveless marriage with a barren wife. At some point he took a mistress. Called 'Mary' according to family tradition, the author suspects it was Mary Kelly, who certainly lived in Wales for a time. When the doctor moved to London, he installed her in a flat near Cleveland Street. Later, he had a change of heart and returned his attentions to his wife, leaving Kelly to fend for herself.

The murders are said to have been committed in the doctor's quest for greater understanding of the workings of the female reproductive organs which he believed would help him to solve the problem of female infertility. This, in turn, would make his name and help his wife to bear children. Williams sought out victims. These he found among the prostitutes he'd treated at a workhouse infirmary in Whitechapel where he did charitable work (the author makes several leaps to explain the lack of records recording the doctor's attendance there, despite existing attendance records for the period showing otherwise). Needless to say, Kelly's death is again the conclusion of his crimes. Into this butchery the author inserts his theory's only Masonic reading, tying in two passages from Leviticus concerning making a 'trespass sacrifice' for 'his sin which he hath sinned'. After this holocaust, Williams turned his back on London and returned to Wales, attempting to ensure his reputation survived untarnished by founding the National Library of Wales in Aberystwyth.

A surgical knife discovered along with the doctor's papers is claimed to match the weapon dimensions estimated during the autopsies. DNA tests are mooted but, as with Sickert, the question remains: to compare against what, exactly?

A Policeman

Fingered by Simon Whitechapel in 'Guts 'N' Roses – Jack the Ripper, Heliogabalus and Meteorites' (2001) Published in *Fortean Studies Volume 7*

...or at the least, someone disguised as a policeman. Whitechapel's (sic) esoteric theory, involving a dark sacrificial ritual to destroy the world, concludes by suggesting the possibility of the Ripper hiding in plain sight. Appearing to be a policeman, the Ripper could approach his victims and could be bloodspattered without attracting suspicion. The more police were drafted into the area, the easier it was for such a disguised Ripper to operate.

There are, of course, many other theories. If you haven't got enough to choose from already, what about the escaped gorilla theory? Or the Fenian seeking to destabilise the government? There are Ripper theories to suit every taste, no matter how strange. There are probably even stranger ones still waiting to be realised. For all the versions of the truth that are flying around out there one question remains: Would we know the absolute truth if we saw it?

Ripping Yarns

"I stopped being interested in Jack the Ripper when it became a cottage industry."

Tom Cullen, author of *Autumn of Terror*

Books

There continues to be a steady stream of theories and factual histories of the Ripper murders – many of these have been listed along with their suspects, or in the bibliography. A similar unstinting flow issues from the fiction market. To list all the titles would be a task beyond the length of this book, so we hope that this brief overview will be of some help.

Ripper historians, however sensationalist, were no slouches when it came to getting into print. G Purkess' *The Whitechapel Murders: Or The Mysteries of the East End* was the first into print, published before Mary Kelly had even been murdered, and was billed as 'a thrilling romance story'. Although the four-page broadsheet 'Jack the Ripper at Work Again' published on 9 November 1888 soon brought the readers up to date.

Not to be outdone, fictional accounts of the Ripper began to appear with equal speed. John Francis Brown's *The Curse Upon Mitre Square* AD 1520–1888 was followed hot on the heels by Anon's 'In the Slaughteryard' (a chapter in *The Adventures of The Adventurers' Club*) in which the Ripper turned cop-killer. There were also policeman's reveries, such as those written by 'Detective Warren' and George Pinkerton, founder of the detective agency, both published in 1889. While Ripper texts continued to be produced, readers had to wait until 1911 for the first truly popular novel based on the case. Inspired by Walter Sickert's tale (see above) Marie Belloc Lowndes' *The Lodger* was first published in short-story form in *McClure's Magazine*, and later the same year in novel form. It continues to be reprinted to this day. Simply told, the mysterious Mr Sleuth rents a room from the Buntings. The Buntings begin to suspect their lodger's nightly outings and fear that he might be the Ripper...

Ripper theory had died down noticeably by the early 1900s with Carl Muusmann (1908) and Leonard Matters (1928) the honourable exceptions. It wasn't really until Donald McCormick's *The Identity of Jack the Ripper*, along with Daniel Farson's BBC documentary in 1959, that the post-war Ripper theory industry got under way. In the fictional world, however, the Ripper flourished. In pulp novels such as *Death Walks In Eastrepps* by Francis Beeding (1931) and short stories like Thomas Burke's grisly 'The Hands of Mr Ottermole', Jack haunted readers throughout the war.

1945 saw the publication of Robert Bloch's 'Yours Truly, Jack the Ripper' – a tale of Jack living in Chicago in the 1940s. First published in the king of pulp magazines *Weird Tales*, this story is Bloch at his best – economical, surprising and never without that streak of sardonic humour that marked much of his better work. Adaptations, for comics, radio and television, followed and the story remains one of the most widely-anthologised of Bloch's work.

Robert Bloch remains somewhat of a touchstone when

considering the Ripper's fictional career. He wrote *The Will to Kill* (1954) in which the protagonist believes that he is responsible for a series of crimes that echo the Whitechapel Murders. In 1967 he contributed the Ripper-in-the-future story 'A Toy for Juliette' to Harlan Ellison's monumental science fiction anthology *Dangerous Visions*, which tells of a sadistic young woman's responsibility for many of the notable disappearances throughout history. Unfortunately, the year 1888 means nothing to her and she comes to a satisfactory end. Bloch's last work on the Ripper was set in 1888. *The Night of the Ripper* (1984) follows a young doctor and a dyspeptic Inspector Abberline as they attempt to track Jack. They eventually find him to be Dr Pedachenko and a female assistant. One of the least satisfying of Bloch's psychological thrillers, it has occasional flashes of wit and reasonable pacing, but cannot hold a candle to his short stories. That said, his ear for Cockney dialogue is still better than the Dick-van-Dyke-isms trotted out in Donald McCormick's *The Identity of Jack the Ripper*.

Outside of the penny dreadfuls capitalising on the Ripper crimes, there have been plenty of fictional attempts to explore the Autumn of Terror. Theodora Benson's *In the Fourth Ward* chillingly relates the real-life killing in Manhattan of the prostitute known as 'Old Shakespeare'. Ray Russell's excellent *Sagittarius* (1962) proposes the Ripper crimes to be perpetrated by Edward Hyde. Hyde in turn has sired a son, who might be responsible for even worse. There was the romance novel *Nine Bucks Row* (1973, aka *Susannah Beware*) by TE Huff, in which a young woman suspects the man she is falling in love with is none other than Jack. Anne Perry's *Pentecost Alley* (1996) had her protagonist wracked with guilt over the possibility that the wrong man was hanged for being the Ripper, especially as he seems to have returned. Anthony Boucher's *A Kind of Madness* (1972) proposes that the Ripper fell victim to the notorious French murderers Michael Eyraud and Gabrielle Bompard, warming up for the murder of solicitor Marcel Gouffé that would bring them notoriety.

Other stories, such as Gardner Fox's *Terror over London* (1957), John Brooks Barry's *The Michaelmas Girls* (1975) and Richard Gordon's *The Private Life of Jack the Ripper* (1980) contained fairly straightforward fictionalised retellings of the murders combined with surprise revelations, usually safely placed within the whodunnit formula. Richard Gordon, creator of the *Doctor in the House* series, built his novel upon solid research about Victorian medical practices. The plot itself is nothing special but there are salutary and disgusting revelations in the background.

The Ripper became the crime and horror writer's equivalent of the dread 'dead pet/living pet' story in sitcoms: something reliable that you could turn to in times of creative hardship. Nowhere is this more apparent than in the countless crime titles in which a serial killer either kills in the same style as the Ripper or is gifted a similar nickname, from Edgar Lustgarten's *A Case to Answer* (1947) to Martina Cole's *Ladykiller* (1993), Rippers of one kind or another are everywhere.

Those of primary interest are Colin Wilson's *Ritual in the Dark* (1960) and *The Killer* (1970). Both portray modern-day Jacks in Wilson's densely-packed prose style and focus on his continuing fascination with the Ripper case. Another title worth tracking down is Fredric Brown's *The Screaming Mimi*

(1949), where an alcoholic reporter is on the trail of a Ripper in Chicago who is killing off showgirls. It was limply filmed in 1958 by Gerd Oswald. However, it also formed the backbone of Dario Argento's classic *giallo*, *The Bird with the Crystal Plumage* (1970).

Although he offered occasional unsolicited advice on the Ripper murders, Sir Arthur Conan Doyle never put his most famous creation to work in tracking Jack down. However, other authors have been only too keen to send Sherlock Holmes down murky East End streets. At a rough estimate, Holmes and the Ripper have crossed paths on at least twenty occasions. From Anon's *Jack El Destripador* to Michael Dibdin's *The Last Sherlock Holmes Story* (1978), Holmes has deducted and deducted again, but they keep bringing him back to have another go. Ellery Queen teamed up with Sherlock in *A Study in Terror* (1966). Barry Roberts' *Sherlock Holmes and the Royal Flush* (1998) matched Holmes against Dr Tumblety. John Sladek's *Black Aura* (1974) suggested Jack was Dr Watson. He wasn't alone – both Holmes and Conan Doyle have been implicated in other novels. And if Holmes' solutions aren't satisfactory then there have always been others to have a go. Mycroft Holmes, Professor Moriarty, Inspector Lestrade, Irene Adler and even Holmes' 'sister', Charlotte, have all had their own Ripper-hunting stories told. In fact, the only character who doesn't seem to have tracked the Ripper is Mrs Hudson... Now why would that be? Surely not...

Alternative views of the Ripper case have been rarer but often better. Harlan Ellison's sequel to Robert Bloch's 'A Toy for Juliette', 'The Prowler in the City at the Edge of the World' (1967) not only offers another suspect for our consideration but throws our voyeurism back in our face as Jack, the eternal outsider, becomes both a sociological experiment and a cheap vicarious thrill for a future society. Ramsey Campbell's hallucinatory *Jack's Little Friend* (1975) proposes a symbiotic relationship that would give David Attenborough nightmares. Patrice Chaplin's *By Flower and Dean Street* (1976) has Jack and Elizabeth Stride possess a modern-day couple who meet in the eponymous street. Peter Ackroyd's atmospheric *Dan Leno and the Limehouse Golem* (1994) features a similar run of crimes almost ten years before the Ripper with a disappointingly predictable ending. Jack headed out West in Richard Laymon's *Savage* (1993), followed by a young boy. Iain Sinclair's *White Chappell, Scarlet Tracings* (1987) tells, in Sinclair's queasily elliptical style, of a group of seedy modern-day second-hand booksellers tracking the Ripper in his William Gull identity. Jack rubbed shoulders with the Vampire King in Kim Newman's splendid *Anno Dracula* (1992) and again in Roger Zelazny's experimental *A Night in the Lonesome October* (1993).

There have been books of poems, several plays and parodies about the Ripper crimes. Jack continues to surface in likely and unlikely places. He has met Doctor Who's Doctor on at least two occasions: *The Pit* (1993) by Neil Penswick and *Matrix* (1998) by Robert Perry and Mike Tucker. In Philip José Farmer's *A Feast Unknown* (1969) Lord Grandrith, a character not at all dissimilar to Tarzan, reveals that the Ripper was his father!

Comics

Graphic violence meets graphic art. Jack has sporadically appeared in comics. He has been the subject of one-off EC-style shockers in horror anthology comics such as *Asylum*, *Creepy* and *The House of Mystery*. He has had guest appearances in longer running series such as Grant Morrison's *Doom Patrol* (issues 23–34, [1989]), Dark Horse comics' *Predator Nemesis* (1997 – spin-off from the Schwarzenegger movie) and DC/Vertigo's *Hellblazer* (the cheerfully seditious 'Royal Blood' 1992, issues 52–55). He has pitted his wits against Judge Dredd ('Night of the Ripper!') Batman ('Gotham by Gaslight', 1989), Wonder Woman ('Amazonia') and even the Justice League of America ('Island of Doctor Moreau') in the incarnation of an orang-utan (shades of Poe). In the four-part *Blood of the Innocents* (1986) by Rickey Shanklin, Mark Wheatley and Marc Hempel, Jack is Prince Eddy, battling with both syphilis and the recently arrived Count Dracula.

The best Ripper comics by far are those by Alan Moore and Eddie Campbell, and Rick Geary. Rick Geary's *Jack the Ripper* (1995) is part of his ongoing *A Treasury of Victorian Murder* series and tells the case from the viewpoint of a Victorian gentleman who relates the case as it was revealed through the press to the public. Geary's slightly soft-looking people and off-kilter framing work wonders for the story and manage to make it feel quite fresh again. Alan Moore and Eddie Campbell's *From Hell* appeared sporadically between 1991 and 1998 in eleven issues published by Tundra and then Kitchen Sink Press. Adopting Stephen Knight's theory from *Jack the Ripper: The Final Solution*, Moore and

Campbell breathe new life into every aspect and character involved in the Ripper crimes. They use the Ripper case to explore every facet of Victorian society and 'the man who was midwife to the 20th Century', his slaughter ushering us into a new century of new horrors. *From Hell*'s final chapter, 'Dance of the Gull-Catchers', which dissects the whole history of Ripperology, should be set reading for anyone interested in the crimes or considering their own final solution.

Films

Farmer Spudd and His Missus Take a Trip to Town (1915, director JVL Leigh) is the first supposed cinematic sighting of the Ripper. The riotously-named Spudd (and presumably, his missus) apparently encounters the Ripper in waxwork form at Madame Tussaud's. Other Wax Rippers were to appear. *Das Wachsfigurenkabinett* (1924, Paul Leni) featured William Dieterle as a young poet hired to write stories about the waxworks and Werner Krauss as the Ripper, coming to life and pursuing him through his dreams in the third and most Expressionist of the three segments. *Terror at the Wax Museum* (1973, George Fenady) featured John Carradine and Ray Milland in a badly-written effort where a Jack the Ripper waxwork might just be committing murders (it's all right, it's not).

The Lodger – A Story of the London Fog (1926)

Director: Alfred Hitchcock. Cast: Ivor Novello, June, Marie Ault, Arthur Chesney

The first (silent) screen outing for Marie Belloc Lowndes' novel. Hitchcock considered this to be his first proper film. Ivor Novello plays the young man suspected of being the Ripper by his landlady. Hitchcock had wanted an ambivalent ending, but Novello was a big enough star for the producers to insist that he must be innocent. The other adaptations were *The Lodger* (1932, Maurice Elvey), a sound version, again featuring Novello in the lead, *The Lodger* (1944, John Brahm) which had Laird Cregar turn out to be the Ripper and *The Man in the Attic* (1953, Hugo Fregonese) which had Jack Palance as the sinister lodger, who is eventually tracked by his fingerprints (something the police in 1888 were still pooh-poohing) and drowns himself. Case closed.

Although based on a BBC feature written by Margery Allingham, *Room to Let* (1949, Godfrey Grayson) was similar in story, featuring Valentine Dyall as the strange lodger and Jimmy Hanley as a nosy (and irritating) reporter. It was one of the first films from the fledgling Hammer studio and was co-scripted by John Gilling.

Die Büsche Der Pandora (1929) (aka *Pandora's Box*)

Director: GW Pabst. Cast: Louise Brooks, Fritz Kortner, Franz Lederer, Gustav Diessl

Adapted from Franz Wedekind's plays *Erdgeist* and *Die Büsche Der Pandora*, it follows the fall of pharmacist's daughter, Lulu (Brooks) through murder and prostitution to her fatal encounter with Jack the Ripper, the Thanatos to her Eros. The plays were refilmed as *Lulu* aka *No Orchids for Lulu* (1962, Rolf Thiele, Nadja Tiller as Lulu), *Lulu* (1978, Ronald Chase, Elisa Leonelli) and (surprise) *Lulu* (1980, Walerian

Borowczyk, Ann Bennent). The plays themselves have been staged on many occasions – in London most recently with Anna Friel earning middling reviews for her Lulu. None of them have achieved the iconic status that Brooks managed back in 1929.

The Ripper has had cameos in other films. GW Pabst's 1930s adaptation of Brecht and Weill's *The Threepenny Opera* and the 1963 version (director Wolfgang Staudte) with Sammy Davis Jr and Gert Frobe (of course I'm serious) had their Mack the Knife. Marcel Carné's *Drôle de Drame* (1937) poked fun at English society and featured a Ripper-like character. There is allegedly a Ripper sub-plot in the dreadful-sounding porno comedy *The Groove Room* (1963, Vernon Becker, it has plenty of other titles) featuring Diana Dors. Played by Sir John Mills in *Deadly Advice* (2003), Jack tries to help Jane Horrocks bump off her mother. Peter O' Toole played a demented aristocrat adopting the persona of Jack the Ripper in *The Ruling Class* (1971, Peter Medak). Sterling Hayden's deranged general in Stanley Kubrick's *Dr Strangelove* (1964) was named 'Jack D Ripper' and caused more mayhem than his namesake could ever have achieved. The real Jack appeared through a mirror, fraudulently acquired by David Warner in 'The Gatecrasher' segment of the Amicus portmanteau horror, *From Beyond the Grave* (1973, Kevin Connor). Needless to say, Warner ends up doing Jack's dirty work.

Jack the Ripper (1958)

Directors: Robert S Baker, Monty Berman. Cast: Eddie Byrne, Lee Patterson, Ewen Solon, John Le Mesurier

'London 1888' reads the opening subtitle, and that's about all they bother to get right. The Ripper turns out to be the VD-crazed surgeon who's got a down on whores. Rumbled by the American detective (he's on vacation), Jack hides in a lift shaft and gets crushed. Some prints of this sprang into Technicolor at this point. As a horror movie it's a bit plodding and, despite the running time of 86 minutes, still feels padded out with endless scenes of can-can dancers' bottoms.

Other attempts vaguely circled around proper retellings: *Das Ungeheuer von London City* (1964, Edwin Zbonek) finds an actor playing Jack the Ripper who is immediately suspected when the murders start up again. Low-budget master Lindsay Shonteff weighed in with *Evil Is...* (1969, aka *Night After Night After Night*) in which Jack May (Nelson Gabriel in *The Archers*) is a judge who turns out to be (gasp) a Jack the Ripper-style murderer. *Jack El Destripador de Londres* (1971) was a standard ham-fisted Paul Naschy vehicle. The Spanish exploitation-movie king finds himself under suspicion when the Ripper starts up again. But it's not him. Klaus Kinski was him, but then you'd have guessed that, in *Jack the Ripper* (1976, Jesus Franco). A full-blooded retelling in the style you'd expect from Jesus Franco, it's still dreadful.

Dr Jekyll and Sister Hyde (1971)

Director: Roy Ward Baker. Cast: Ralph Bates, Martine Beswick, Gerald Sim

The first of Hammer's two Ripper tales, released in 1971. This one starts with the premise of male Jekyll (Bates) turning into the female Hyde (Beswick). To continue his experiments Jekyll needs female hormones. Hyde obliges by taking some from the local prostitutes.

Robert Louis Stevenson had written *The Strange Case of Dr Jekyll and Mr Hyde* in 1886. At the time of the Ripper murders it was being successfully staged at the Lyceum. Richard Mansfield's performance in the lead(s) was so enthusiastic that it drew criticism for inciting serial murder. Its audiences fell and the play closed early. Since then, many screen adaptations of Stevenson's novel have included elements of the Ripper crimes. Most blatant was *Edge of Sanity* (1988, Gerard Kikoine) which starred an ill-looking Anthony Perkins and Victorian prostitutes who all seemed to be dressed for a Madonna lookalike contest.

Hands of the Ripper (1971)

Director: Peter Sasdy. Cast: Eric Porter, Angharad Rees, Jane Merrow, Keith Bell

One of the last great Hammer films. Rees plays the daughter of Jack the Ripper driven to kill by certain external stimuli. Porter is the psychiatrist who attempts to cure her. It all ends badly in St Paul's Cathedral. A notably cinematic and cine-literate film, not even marred by the photographic backdrop of the Whispering Gallery at the climax (Sasdy and his crew weren't allowed into the cathedral).

In the seventies attempts were also made to cross-pollinate the Ripper with standard American genres: *A Knife for the Ladies* (1973, Larry Spengler) was a horror-western with the odd-eyed Jack Elam; *Black the Ripper* (1975, Frank R Salteri) was a proposed low-end blaxploitation movie that possibly never got made. They both sound as good as the lame Bob Hope vehicle *Here Come the Girls* (1953, Claude Binyon) where ol' ski-slope nose is accused of being Jack the Slasher but turns out not to be. The songs are no better than the plot.

Murder by Decree (1978)

Director: Bob Clark. Cast: Christopher Plummer, James Mason, David Hemmings, Genevieve Bujold, Anthony Quayle, John Gielgud, Frank Finlay, Donald Sutherland

Clark's movie adapts the theory proposed in John Lloyd and Elwyn Jones' *The Ripper Files* (itself based on the BBC drama-documentary) – the same one that would fuel Stephen Knight's book. Sherlock Holmes (Plummer) and Dr Watson (Mason, a well-rounded portrait) are summoned once more to solve the Ripper murders and stumble upon a nest of corruption (illegitimate royal children, blackmailing prostitutes, Masonic cover-up). The drama is well judged but the pride of the film is its set design and cinematography – rendering the East End streets as a surreal labyrinth of menacing alleyways and dark, dark recesses where corruption and terror hang in the air. The film has some truly disturbing scenes, such as when Holmes stumbles upon Spivey and Slade at Mary Kelly's. With so much going for it, its convictions falter. Gull and Netley become Dr Thomas Spivey and William Slade. Anthony Quayle (Lord Salisbury) is only referred to as 'The Prime Minister'. Most unforgivably, after a very lengthy explanation at the climax, Holmes goes completely against his character and lets the Freemasons off the hook.

The Ripper had already met Holmes on screen before in *A Study in Terror* (1965, James Hill) with John Neville as Holmes and Donald Houston as Watson. This is a fairly poor film which bumbles along tiresomely (not unlike Houston), throwing in some gory moments and fogbound sets. The cast's obvious uncertainty as to how straight they should play it means that there are times it almost teeters into 'Carry on' territory. Barbara Windsor as one of the victims doesn't help.

Time After Time (1979)

Director/Writer: Nicholas Meyer. Cast: Malcolm McDowell, David Warner, Mary Steenburgen

Proof that you can't keep a good Ripper down, Meyer's entertaining and bloody movie proposes another reason why the murders stopped: time travel. Warner's Ripper, chased by the police, escapes using a time machine designed and built by his friend HG Wells (McDowell). Projected into modern San Francisco, Jack sets about his trade once more, with Wells in hot pursuit.

Other Ripper-thru-time movies came from the TV movie *Bridge Across Time* (1985, EW Swackhamer, aka *Arizona Ripper*, *Terror on London Bridge*). David Hasselhoff and Adrienne Barbeau have a hard time when they discover that the Ripper has somehow been transported to Arizona along with London Bridge (you saw the titles, you knew what to expect). William F Nolan rewrote his script as the short story, 'The Final Stone', which included a different identity for the Ripper. *The Ripper* (1985, Christopher Lewis) was an exploitation cheapie featuring effects and a cameo appearance by Tom Savini. The Ripper's ring passes on his evil to a modern-day college professor. Screaming women ensue.

Sadly, these two were just three years shy of the Ripper Centenary, thus missing the boat. *Jack's Back* (1988, Rowdy Herrington) was dead on time and played upon genuine public concerns that some maniac would see fit to celebrate in the spirit of the season. Or, perhaps, the real Jack would re-emerge. Not in this he didn't. James Spader plays a struggling medico in the poor end of town. Women are dying in a Jack the Ripper style. Spader figures it out but the Ripper kills him. Enter Spader's twin brother, err... James Spader, to flush out the killer. As a cash-in it's pretty unfocussed but there are some neat twists and turns to the cheerfully convoluted plot. And it's got two James Spaders. *Ripper Man* (1996) had none, instead featuring Timothy Bottoms as a modern-day hypno-eyed psychopath being chased by cop-on-the-edge Mike 'son of Chuck' Norris. Mike's fighting style isn't much; instead he seems to have inherited his father's ability to pick scripts.

Jack the Ripper (1988)

Director: David Wickes. Cast: Michael Caine, Armand Assante, Jane Seymour, Ray McAnally, Lewis Collins, Susan George

At the 'quality' drama end of the market – or rather the 'mid-quality, mid-evening' drama end – there was Euston Films' self-proclaimed 'proper' telling of the story of Jack the Ripper. Well, okay. The three one-hour episodes were appropriately mounted, with newspaper-wielding urchins, horses, carts and the occasional odd-looking bicycle to the fore. However, the Vigilance Committees are played like torch-bearing lynch mobs out of a Frankenstein movie, and there is an odd focus on Assante's Richard Mansfield as a prime suspect. His Hyde might have been good but I would be more concerned about how he got hold of 1980s bladder effects than whether he was the Ripper.

Along with the usual 'faces' of 1980s mid-range drama (Susan George as Catharine Eddowes!), Michael Caine attacks his role of the reportedly mild-mannered and reserved Inspector Abberline with both fists. Permanently annoyed and shouting at everyone in sight, Caine's Abberline always seems to be on the verge of chinning Lewis Collins. It starts to become uncomfortably possible that Abberline will lose it completely, march out into the street and yell: 'Oy! You, bloody Ripper! Leave those bloody prostitutes alone!' On the plus side, the plot unrolls at a decent gallop over the film's worst offences.

Taking more liberties with history than David Irving, Janet Meyers' *The Ripper* (1997) features a fictional copper (Patrick Bergin's Beethoven-haired Inspector Hanson) and a fictional prostitute (Gabrielle Anwar's Oirish washerwoman Florry Lewis) hot on the trail of Jack as Heir-to-the-Throne, Samuel West's barking Prince Eddy. Mind you, 'barking' is a relative term: Michael York's Sir Charles Warren (one of the few 'real' people in it) is a fuzzy old buffer more interested in pairing off his protégée (Hanson) than catching the Ripper. If you've stayed with us this far then you'll flinch like we did when Hanson shows Florry Mary Kelly's murder photo just after the 'double-header' (itself bumped up the running order). By now, it should be clear that we've no problem with fictional retellings of the case but... the muddle! Historical verisimilitude is attempted with slops being chucked out of East End windows and the most men with absurd facial hair filling the screen since *Gettysburg* (1993). The line (delivered completely straight), 'He may be insane but... lovely penmanship', deserves some kind of recognition. Although, for the life of us, we couldn't say what kind.

From Hell (2001)

Directors: Albert Hughes, Allen Hughes. Cast: Johnny Depp, Heather Graham, Ian Holm, Robbie Coltrane, Ian Richardson

Filmed mainly in Prague, the troubled production finally hit the screens with a hole in its heart. Johnny Depp played Inspector Abberline as a *fin de siècle* occultist a few notches more experienced than his Ichabod Crane in Sleepy Hollow (see the lovingly-filmed scene where Abberline fixes himself a glass of absinthe). His romance with Heather Graham's Mary Kelly (apparently voiced by Dick Van Dyke) leads up to one of the most jaw-droppingly cynical *deus ex machina* ever foisted on the movie-going public. Finally, the Whitechapel Murders gets a happy ending. Thanks, Hollywood, that's just what it was missing. Bloody, stylish and with a credible recreation of the Whitechapel streets, *From Hell* misses the point of Moore and Campell's creation by a mile. This isn't really its fault. You try pitching Fox a lengthy dissection of the Victorian era and the impending birth of a new century. What we end up with is a flashier version of *Murder by Decree* with the real people reinstated. Arguably the most noticeable lack is the filtering of the murders through Gull's spiralling messiah complex, lending them a horrifying grandeur. Instead, Ian Holm's Gull has little to do except some weary verbal-jousting with Depp, and seems to be killing simply to get some screen time... we'll stop moaning. We should know the drill by now. We've seen *Swamp Thing*, after all.

More recently, John Eyre's *Ripper* (2003) is an efficient slasher movie with a killer whose m.o. echoed Jack's. Sort of. Students of a forensic science class (whose initials match those of the original victims) end up with their insides outside. *Ripper* makes some interesting points about contemporary consumption of true crime narratives while supplying the requisite twists and jolts. The increasingly cadaverous Jurgen Prochnow appears as a red herring. Not literally, you understand.

If you've ever wondered what a horror movie made by a bunch of goths would look like, then *I Am the Ripper* (2004) might give you an idea. An amateur French cast get killed, come back to life, and get killed again by a hooded figure who may be Death or possibly Skeletor. Exactly how Jack fits into the story may be just the result of an opportunistic retitling for this incomprehensible mess. At one point someone does appear wearing a top hat and a cape but by then our brains had shut down our retinas as a precautionary measure and we knew no more.

Television

Just as he does in crime books, the Ripper often crops up in TV series to fairly average and unimaginative effect. So far, these appearances have included:

The New Adventures of Sherlock Holmes (1955)

The Big Story (1956)

Alfred Hitchcock Presents (1957)

The Veil (1958), episode titled 'Jack the Ripper'

Cimarron City (1958) 'Knife in the Darkness'. Western series, episode written and disowned, after directorial tampering, by Harlan Ellison

Thriller (1961). 'Yours Truly, Jack the Ripper', from the Robert Bloch story. Series hosted by Boris Karloff

The Green Hornet (1966) 'Alias the Scarf'. Crime-fighting superhero stuff with Van Johnson and Bruce Lee

Star Trek (1967) 'Wolf in the Fold'. Scripted by Robert Bloch

The Avengers (1969) 'Fog'. Linda Thorson-era episode, directed by John Hough

The Sixth Sense (1972) 'With Affection, Jack the Ripper'

Kolchak the Night Stalker (1974) 'The Ripper'. Darren McGavin's reporter finally electrocutes immortal Ripper in Chicago

Fantasy Island (1980) 'With Affection, Jack the Ripper'. 'Boss! Boss! It's Leather Apron!'

Sliders (1997) 'Murder Most Foul'

Babylon 5 (1997) 'Comes the Inquisitor'

Plus Jack has had cameo appearances in shows such as *Dave Allen At Large* and *Till Death Us Do Part*. And how could we forget the sublimely daft Spike Milligan-scripted *The Phantom Raspberry of Old London Town* in *The Two Ronnies* (1976)?

And Jack the Ripper? Who was he really? After nearly a century of speculation, *Amazon Women on the Moon* (1987, Joe Dante, John Landis, Peter Horton, Carl Gottlieb, Robert K Weiss) puts forward its own final solution: the Loch Ness Monster.

Ripper Haunts

A visit to the True Crime section of your nearest first- or second-hand bookshop cannot fail to yield many books about saucy Jack, but below we list a bloody few to whet your appetite.

History/Sourcebooks

The following titles cannot be underestimated in their importance in accurately chronicling the Ripper case. However, even here, variations can occur and the dedicated Ripper reader will want to compare:

Sugden, Philip, *The Complete History of Jack the Ripper*, London: Robinson, 1995, Paperback, 542 pages, £8.99, ISBN 1854874160.

The definitive book on Jack the Ripper, no argument. Every single detail of the murders, the victims and the investigation has been meticulously researched and presented in an extremely readable form. Although Sugden leans slightly towards George Chapman as a suspect, he resists any attempt at a final solution. Highly recommended.

Rumbelow, Donald, *The Complete Jack the Ripper*, London: Penguin, 1988, Paperback, 310 pages, £8.99, ISBN 0140173951.

For those in slightly more of a hurry, ex-copper Rumbelow's book is the thing. A well-presented overview of the case that, once again, resists the temptation to speculate. Rumbelow also works as master of ceremonies on the best of the Ripper Walks.

Evans, Stewart P and Skinner, Keith (eds), *The Ultimate Jack the Ripper Sourcebook*, London: Robinson, 2000, Hardback, 692 pages, £25, ISBN 1841192252.

A necessary purchase for any budding Ripperologist, Evans and Skinner have compiled the definitive reference book on the Ripper crimes. It contains all Home Office and Scotland Yard files on the case, plus available inquest transcripts. There are also reproductions of the first Ripper letters, the Macnaghten Memoranda et al. The truth is in here, some-where...

Begg, Paul, Fido, Martin and Skinner, Keith, *The Jack the Ripper A-Z*, London: Headline, 1996, Paperback, 522 pages, £8.99, ISBN 0747255229.

Another reference work without which the Ripperologist would be nothing. Despite some factual errors (which encourage you to do your own research – go on), this is an exhaustively compiled volume containing information on every aspect and person involved in the case.

Evans, Stewart and Skinner, Keith, *Jack the Ripper: Letters from Hell*, Stroud: Sutton, 2004, Paperback, 306 pages, £12.99, ISBN 075093770X.

This excellently-produced volume provides transcripts and

reproductions of many of the missives that bombarded press and police during and since the crimes. So did Sickert write them all?

Begg, Paul, *Jack the Ripper: The Facts*, London: Robson, 2006, Paperback, 560 pages, £8.99, ISBN: 1861058705.

As well-referenced as Begg's previous *Jack the Ripper: The Definitive History*, *The Facts* contains less social history but far more exhaustive detail about the case. The choice between this and the Sugden is really down to personal preference.

Curtis, L Perry, *Jack the Ripper and the London Press*, Yale: Yale University Press, 2001, Hardback, 320 pages, £25.00, ISBN 0300088728.

Interesting study of the press's relationship with the Ripper crimes. A little dry in places with an occasionally faltering argument but full marks for a different approach.

Bibliographies

Both of the following contain exhaustive listings of the vast range of factual and fictional titles available:

Kelly, Alexander and Sharp, David, *Jack the Ripper: A Bibliography and Review of the Literature*, London: Association of Assistant Librarians, 1994, Paperback, 176 pages, £6, ISBN 0900092904.
Strachan, Ross, *The Jack the Ripper Handbook: A Reader's Companion*, UK: Great Scot Services, 1999, Paperback, 188 pages, £12, ISBN 0953694909.

Fiction

The following are worth tracking down for excellent speculative explorations of the Ripper case. While the first is out of print, the other two should be easier to get hold of.

Parry, Michel (ed), *Jack the Knife: Tales of Jack the Ripper*, London: Mayflower, 1975, Paperback, 160 pages, 50p, ISBN 583125026. Contains stories by Joseph F Pumilia, Hume Nisbet, Marie Belloc Lowndes, Anon, Anthony Boucher, R Chetwynd-Hayes, Philip José Farmer, Robert Bloch, Ramsey Campbell and Harlan Ellison
(nb: between two anthologies called *Jack the Ripper* [1988, Futura Books, edited by Gardner Dozis and Susan Casper and 2004, i-books, edited by Martin Greenburg] most of *Jack the Knife*'s stories are reprinted.)

Geary, Rick, *A Treasury of Victorian Murder: Jack the Ripper*, US: NBM Publishing, 1995, Hardback, 64 pages, $15.95, ISBN 1561631248

Moore, Alan and Campbell, Eddie, *From Hell*, UK: Knockabout Comics, 2000, Paperback, 576 pages, £24.99, ISBN: 0861661419

The Whitechapel Web

It'll come as no surprise that there are quite a few websites covering the Ripper's crimes. Of these, those most worth a visit are:

www.casebook.org
'The Daddy'. Easily the best Ripper site, this has sections

devoted to the victims, suspects, press reports etc. Nicely laid out with special 'dissertations' on various aspects of the case, any budding Ripperologist should make this their first net stop.

www.accomodata.co.uk/jack.htm
Subtly illustrated pages with the basics of the case summarised, this site makes a good Ripper digest for the curious.

www.hollywoodripper.com
The ideal site if you want to find out more about Jack's celluloid outings. Plenty of trivia and posters liven up the site, and there's even a PDF of *The Curse Upon Mitre Square* (1888) – a nice touch.

Jack's Little Friends

Ripperana is a quarterly magazine, edited by Nick Warren, which covers many aspects of true crime but focuses particularly on Jack, including new titbits and theories surrounding the case. Subscriptions £6 (UK), $15 (US) per year, payable by cheques (UK: payable to NP Warren), or currency (US) to: 16 Copperfield Way, Pinner, HA5 5RY.

London Walks' Jack the Ripper Haunts is the original and definitely the best Ripper walk. It starts every night from Tower Hill Underground Station at 7.30pm (and Saturday afternoons at 3.00pm). Your host for Sundays, Mondays, Tuesdays and alternate Fridays is usually author Donald Rumbelow. £5 charge (£3.50 for senior citizens and students, under 15s free with an adult). Call 0207 624 3978 for more info.

For those with a really strong stomach, try the impressively accurate Jack the Ripper Experience at The London Dungeon, Tooley Street, London, SE1. It's open 10am-5.30pm (5pm in winter) every day of the year. Entry fee: £10.95 (adults), £9.50 (students), £6.50 (kids under 14 and senior citizens).

Related Materials

The following titles concern cases of interest to Ripper enthusiasts and are worth reading in their own right:

Bondeson, Jan, *The London Monster – A Sanguinary Tale*, London: Free Association Books, 2000, Paperback, 256 pages, £8.99, ISBN 1853435260.
'Springheeled Jack: To Victorian Bugaboo from Suburban Ghost' by Mike Dash, in Moore, Steve (ed), *Fortean Studies*, *Volume 3*, UK: John Brown Publishing, 1996, Paperback, 384 pages, £19.99, ISBN 1870870824.
Goss, Mike, *The Halifax Slasher: An Urban Terror in the North of England*, UK: Fortean Times Occasional Paper No 3, 1987, Paperback, 56 pages, £2.50, ISSN 02605856.
James, PD and Critchley, TA, *The Maul and the Pear Tree: The Ratcliffe Highway Murders, 1811*, London: Faber and Faber, 2000, Paperback, 274 pages, £8.99, ISBN: 0571202829.

Index